PATTERNS OF LIGHT

Volume 1

Discovering Patterns of Recovery
within the Book of Mormon
and Twelve Step Literature

Colleen C. Harrison

Hearthaven Publishing
12 Step Materials for the LDS Community
HYRUM, UT

Hearthaven Publishing
12 Step Materials for the LDS Community
PO Box 31
Hyrum, UT 84319
www.hearthavenpublishing.com

ISBN: 978-1-930738-23-2

Printed in the United States of America
1 2 3 4 5 6 7 8 9 10 19 18 17 16 15

Acknowledgments

There are three people who have been "the wind beneath my wings" in my Twelve Step journey. Joy S. and Nannette W. have been involved with the dream of creating this LDS Step Study from its inception. They have nourished this work with enthusiasm, faith and trust, contributing many personal insights. And then, there's Karlene B. This woman is the most gifted midwife of the published word a writer could hope for.

These three women are my sisters in Zion—of one heart and one mind, even as I am, to bring recovery and redemption to our fellow Saints.

Table of Contents

How to Use This Book

Patterns of Light, Volume I represents the interweaving of Book of Mormon scriptures and quotations from *Alcoholics Anonymous* (commonly referred to as the *AA Big Book*) and *Twelve Steps and Twelve Traditions* (referred to as the *12 & 12*). This correlation with the scriptures will provide an in-depth study of the principles of recovery found in the Twelve Steps.

Scriptures are arranged in four sets of seven. This book, along with *Patterns of Light, Volume II,* allows you to create a year-long course of study. You may focus on one step each month, or study a different step each week, rotating through all twelve steps four times in the course of a year.

Scripture references for each verse are listed first, so that you can turn to them in your own copy of the Book of Mormon. It is important that you study the verses in their entirety and in context. It is suggested that you obtain copies of *Alcoholics Anonymous* and *Twelve Steps and Twelve Traditions,* so that you may also read the quotes from those books in their entirety.

Other references which you may want to obtain are *The Teachings of the Prophet Joseph Smith* and past issues of the *Ensign*. (Back issues of the *Ensign* may be found at www.lds.org)

Following each scripture reference, you will find thought-provoking commentary and questions to help you apply the principle in the verse to your own life. We recommend that you prayerfully ponder these scriptures, capture* them in your writings, and answer the questions in your permanent journal.

You will find references throughout these booklets to addiction(s), compulsive and/or addictive behavior(s) and other specific behaviors, such as overeating (the primary addiction of the author), compulsive spending, perfectionism, codependency, and so forth. Please feel free to substitute any insurmountable, inescapable problem (crisis) that you may be experiencing in place of these references.

Some readers have found it helpful to mark their scriptures to correlate with the Twelve Steps, using a different color marker for each step. If you wish to do so, you can find a downloadable Scripture Marking Chart at www.shop.hearthavenpublishing.com/freebies.

**See "What Is Capturing?" in the Appendix*

Introduction

Hi! My name is Colleen, and I'm a person who has been challenged by compulsive addictive behaviors most of my life.

Before I go any further, I would like to express my appreciation for this chance to share my experience, strength and hope with you. Thanks for being there for me and blessing me with this opportunity.

The Origin of This Work

I've been in and around Twelve Step groups since 1981, working on my recovery from several forms of severe childhood trauma and the dependencies on compulsive eating, compulsive spending, perfectionism, workaholism, and codependency that resulted from that trauma. I have also struggled to overcome self-worth and self-esteem issues that stem from such childhood experiences and adult choices. It requires a daily dose (and sometimes several doses a day) of spiritual connectedness to sustain a remission from the lies I have inherited and the challenges those incorrect beliefs create for me.

This study guide originally began with my attempt to turn to the scriptures every morning for at least 10–15 minutes, looking for and capturing from verses that verified the principles in the Twelve Steps. (See "What Is Capturing" in the Appendix.)

I focused primarily on the Book of Mormon because President Ezra Taft Benson, who was the prophet of the Church at the time, had stated that the Book of Mormon was *the* book written for *our* time. I theorized that if this were so, then it should be all about recovery. I wondered if I would be able to find these twelve principles validated in the Book of Mormon.

I purchased an inexpensive copy of the Book of Mormon. I wanted to feel free to underline, write in the margins, and generally mark it up with complete abandon to the Spirit that I fully trusted would attend my efforts.

At first, I was a little doubtful. I was positive the word "addiction" was *not* in the Book of Mormon. But as I began to read, I felt as if I had been given a gift of translation. It was as if I were reading with new eyes. I began to see the references to "bondage" as references to the *bondage* of addiction. I saw references to "enemies" as being applicable to my character defects or to my dysfunctional behaviors which had once been my coping devices—addictions and compulsions that had started as my friends but were now on the verge of destroying me.

With just those two transpositions, the Book of Mormon became the ultimate book on addiction and recovery. I read it with an excitement and a hunger and a thirst that I had never felt before.

The Book of Mormon spoke to me, personally. I began to awaken to the truth of Joseph's statement that this book is **"the most correct of any book on earth" (Book of Mormon, Introduction)**. It has truly become the keystone of my spiritual life. And in harmony with the pattern of true principles found in the Twelve Steps,

I had its precepts open to my mind and heart. Through this experimentation upon the word (see **Alma 34:4**), I have been brought nearer to God than I ever imagined possible. It is this harmony that I hope to convey for the blessing of others.

By the time I finished the Book of Mormon, the truth of the Twelve Steps was riveted on my heart—and so was the truth of the Book of Mormon. I realized that the Twelve Steps were a powerful curriculum for studying the Gospel principles in simple, baby steps. This study renewed my witness of Joseph Smith's prophetic calling and of the Church's authenticity.

The Intention of This Work

This in-depth study of the Twelve Steps and their correlation with the Book of Mormon is not intended to take the place of your personal scripture study. It is simply to demonstrate the recovery that is available in the scriptures of the Restoration. It is my intent, hope, and prayer that you will enjoy and rejoice in these offered insights, *and* that you will have many insights of your own as your heart resonates and your mind responds to the insights I've been given to share.

I encourage you to write your thoughts in your personal journal pages, and to add your own references in the spaces provided at the end of each Step's section. Use this book as a starting point on your journey of recovery. Then, with the guidance of the Holy Spirit, transform it into a record of your relationship with the scriptures and with the Lord.

It is my fervent prayer that working through these exercises will introduce everyone who uses them to the truthfulness of both the Book of Mormon and the

Twelve Step model of recovery—and all for the purpose of bringing us to Christ, that we might become perfect through our relationship with Him (see **Moroni 10:32**).

– *Colleen C. Harrison*

Step One

We admitted we were powerless—that our lives had become unmanageable. Admitted that we of ourselves are powerless, nothing without God.

Step One presented quite a hurdle for me when I was first introduced to it—as it does for many Latter-day Saints. *Me? Powerless? Not me!*

After all, I am a child of God, *literally*. That's what the Restoration teaches. God sent me here to prove that I can stand on my own two feet, learn to be a God myself. God is independent. Isn't he?... (see *Teachings of the Prophet Joseph Smith,* 353).

Believe me, if being power-filled and self-sufficient was the end result God wanted to see in me, then my addiction—this desperate, destructive dependency I had on overeating—was convicting me of being the worst failure I could imagine. I needed my addiction to get me through every day of my life. I felt hopeless and powerless, living a life of spiritual bankruptcy created by the "rapacious creditor" of my addiction. (*AA Twelve Steps and Twelve Traditions,* 21; subsequently referred to in this text as *12&12.*)

As I prayed and pondered my way through the Book of Mormon, I found dozens of references to support the idea that we are powerless without God. The harmony between Bill Wilson's life-changing experience and Ammon's words hit my soul with all the power of the principle of **"out of the mouths of two or** [more] **witnesses" (Matthew 18:16; D&C 6:28)**.

> There I humbly offered myself to God, as I then understood Him, to do with me as He would. I placed myself unreservedly under His care and direction. *I admitted for the first time that of myself I was nothing; that without Him I was lost* (*Alcoholics Anonymous,* 13; emphasis added; subsequently referred to in this text as *AA*).

> **Yea, I know that I am nothing; as to my strength I am weak; therefore I will not boast of myself, but I will boast of my God, for in his strength I can do all things… (Alma 26:12).**

And finally from the Pearl of Great Price:

> **Now, for this cause I know that man is nothing, which thing I never had supposed (Moses 1:10).**

I was frankly puzzled and tempted to be frustrated at either myself or the Church. I couldn't figure out how I could have read so many books by church leaders, and attended Seminary, Institute, Education Weeks, Sunday School—and not heard this principle taught! How could a concept so central to the message of the scriptures of the Restoration and to the theology of the Gospel be so unfamiliar in our cultural paradigm?

The following benevolent insight came to me as I prayed to understand:

Such a mindset is understandable, when one places the Latter-day Saints in their historical context. The early history of the Church—their persecution within the United States borders; their flight into the wilderness of the unsettled arid desert regions of the great Intermountain West; their necessity to establish a tradition of intense self-reliance. All of these add up to a relatively insulated and sheltered environment. Steeped in this tradition for over a hundred and fifty years, several generations of Latter-day Saints (speaking of our people as a whole, not as individuals) have often confused the value of temporal independence under God **(D&C 78:14)** with needing to be independent from God.

The following 28 daily exercises weave together the testimony of the Book of Mormon with complementary quotes from the literature of Alcoholics Anonymous, and offer an in-depth study of Step One and the principle of powerlessness. Commentary and thought-provoking questions are included to help liken these concepts to your own recovery. Use the sacred tool of prayerful writing to capture and hold these principles in your heart and to leave a record of your spiritual journey for your children and loved ones who come after you.

Step One—Week One

1.1 Mosiah 3:19—For the natural man is an enemy to God.

This verse goes on to describe what it means for us to become a saint, not through our own works, but through the atonement of Jesus Christ. We must somehow persuade (see **D&C 121:41**) our natural-man self to become **"as a child, submissive, meek, humble, patient, full of love, willing to submit to *all things* which the Lord seeth fit to *inflict* upon** [us], **even as a child doth submit to his father" (Mosiah 3:19; emphasis added).**

> Who cares to admit complete defeat? Practically no one, of course. Every *natural instinct* cries out against the idea of personal powerlessness (*12&12*, 21; emphasis added).

Can you hear the harmony of these two testimonies? I have come to realize that there exists in each of us two selves, or personae. I'm not referring to a pathological condition such as Multiple Personality Disorder. I'm talking about the average person seeking to become whole.

Within each of us is the eternal self, who is not an enemy to God. According to LDS theology, this eternal self exists co-eternally with God, lived with God, and valiantly defended God's truth before this mortality. And then, also within us, is our finite, mortal self—our natural-man self—who came into existence only a number of years ago, and who knows only so much of life as we have been taught in this mortality.

The natural man expresses itself as pride. This pride is a form of "*enmity* toward God… [a] 'hatred toward, hostility to, or a state of opposition'" (Ezra Taft Benson, "Beware of Pride," *Ensign*, May 1989, 4).

It is a rejection of the spiritual and of being led by the Spirit.

The natural man leads us to place our dependency needs on something or someone in this world—the only world we can remember. To become powerless and to see yourself as *nothing without God* is the equivalent of bringing your natural-man self to admit that God exists, that your eternal self exists. It means accepting that your natural-man self is as completely dependent upon God and the eternal self within you as an infant is completely dependent upon his parents.

Application:

Ponder and prayerfully write about how your life has been marked by resistance to being willing to "accept life completely on life's terms" (*AA*, 449).

How has your addiction (or other insurmountable problem) kept you from relying on God and honoring the spiritual life (self) within you?

Have you felt any degree of enmity towards God—or towards the events, circumstances, or people in the life God has allowed you to have? How have feelings of confusion, frustration, or anger contributed to your flight into idolatry (addiction)?

1.2 Mosiah 3:25—Therefore they have *drunk* damnation to their own souls (emphasis added).

Compulsive addictive behaviors include drinking alcohol, overeating, using illegal drugs or abusing legal drugs, using sexual excitement, and indulging in any other addictive substance or behavior. The problem with these behaviors is that they begin small. We often ease into our addiction. Gradually, our use grows, until eventually it is so powerful that it literally damns us by stopping our emotional and spiritual development.

Our relationship with addiction can destroy all our other relationships, like a cancer which robs healthy cells around it of energy and nourishment. Even our physical health can be threatened as we progress from an occasional indulgence, to a habit, to a compulsion, to a degree of self-destructive addiction that begins to possess our soul and influences us to **"shrink from the presence of the Lord" (Mosiah 2:38)**—who is our *only* hope for deliverance. It is as if the addiction takes on a life of its own and perpetuates itself in our minds and hearts.

Application:

Write a very brief (1 or 2 pages, maximum) history of your compulsive addictive behavior. What was it like at first? How much did you indulge in this behavior in the beginning of your relationship with it? How has it progressed?

Have there been periods of remission when you've been able to avoid these behaviors? How have you felt when the behaviors returned? Has it caused you to give up on the Lord? Or have you felt that He must have given up on you?

Does it feel like this behavior pattern has a life of its own? Where might it get that life? (Read **Moroni 7:17** before you answer.)

1.3 Mosiah 4:2—And they had viewed themselves in their own carnal state, even *less than the dust of the earth* (emphasis added).

Remember, these were good, active members of the church who gathered to hear King Benjamin's words and who came to "[view] **themselves in their own carnal state."**

Why less than the dust of the earth? Because the dust of the earth loves and obeys God instantly, spontaneously, trusting Him in all things, while man—even the most devout man—wrestles with the temptation to resist or turn away from God (see **Helaman 12:6** and **2 Nephi 4**).

Each of us must eventually come to a place where we are humble enough to admit that we too are **"less than the dust of the earth."** All of us—whether active church member, less active, inactive, disfellowshipped, or excommunicated—must accept our "devastating [tendency to] weakness and all its consequences," as a stark fact of our mortal existence (*12&12*, 21).

Application:

Ponder and prayerfully write about your feelings and reactions to surrendering to the fact of your own mortal limitations and weaknesses. How does it feel to realize that you have finally discovered the boundaries of your own willpower? Are you grateful to be compelled to be humble and to turn to God? Why or why not?

1.4 Mosiah 24:21—For they were in bondage, and none could deliver them except it were the Lord their God.

Bondage. This is the key concept that originally burst upon my mind and opened my awareness to the beautiful harmony between the Twelve Step program of recovery from addiction and the Book of Mormon. Suddenly, the Book of Mormon's emphasis on wars and battles and people taking each other captive—all the dynamics of life and death struggles—made perfect sense to me. The entire book is a series of metaphors and parables about how people get into bondage and how they get out!

We who have fled into the prisons of addictive or compulsive behavior, driven there by our resentments and regrets, our self-pity and self-will, are also enslaved. As the Book of Mormon and the original literature of Alcoholics Anonymous testify in unison: "We are 100% hopeless, apart from divine help" (*AA*, 43).

There is no power that can deliver us from the bondage of compulsive, addictive behaviors either, except Christ. "Only an act of Providence can remove [them] from us" (*12&12*, 21).

Application:

Ponder and prayerfully write about the battle you have waged with your problem. How many other ways have you tried to deal with or overcome your addiction or problem? List these half measures (*AA*, 59) that may have been good up to a point but which then lost their power to sustain your recovery.

1.5 Mosiah 27:29—My soul hath been redeemed from the gall of bitterness and bonds of iniquity. I was in the darkest abyss;... My soul was racked with eternal torment.

Gall of bitterness? Bonds of iniquity? Darkest abyss? Racked with eternal torment? Have you ever heard a better set of phrases to describe the experience of hitting bottom?

Step One is the establishment of our *absolute need* for God. For most of us, this is not a very pleasant experience. We feel like our mortal weaknesses have sucked us down into the clutches of insanity and the pits of hell.

How paradoxical it is to realize that this bottomed out place of absolute humility is actually the firm bedrock upon which all the other principles of recovery, repentance, and redemption are grounded (see *12&12,* 21).

Application:

Ponder and prayerfully write about one or more of those pits of hell moments, or periods of insanity, in your own darkest abyss experience. This exercise of remembering is not for the sake of further torture, but for the sake of stripping away any layers of denial that may still be covering up our full consciousness of how awful it was—and maybe still is.

Bitterness. Bonds. Iniquity. Darkest abyss. Eternal torment (see **D&C 19:5–12**). How could you use these words to apply to your past? If you feel these words don't apply, you may be one of those who will be spared from having to bottom out because of your willingness to learn these things without being compelled (**Alma 32:16;** *12&12,* 23). Write about the hardest moments you've had, or that you've seen others have.

1.6 Alma 32:13—Because ye are compelled to be humble blessed are ye; for a man sometimes, if he is compelled to be humble, seeketh repentance.

No direct compulsion may be used upon the souls of the children of men by a righteous priesthood holder (see **D&C 121:37 & 41**). Thus, while God (the epitome of a righteous priesthood holder) does not compel us by force, He does allow other influences, such as natural circumstances and consequences, to give us experience. He knows full well that **"wickedness never was happiness" (Alma 41:10)** and that, sooner or later, we will have had enough of the influence of wickedness.

When we reach that point of truth, we will come around, come to our self, and come back to Him—all in the act of seeking repentance.

When we come to Him, we will realize that all of this life's experiences have been orchestrated for this very purpose—to compel, or cause, us to be humble. This humility causes us to seek repentance and to turn to God. When we are turned to Him, *He* is then free to give us all that He has. Our compulsions compel us to be humble or powerless, thus turning our hearts to God.

Application:

Ponder and prayerfully write about the idea that while God does not—in fact, *can* not—compel us, He has created this telestial world so that we can be exposed to good and evil, or rather, to learn what works and what doesn't work. Write about the idea that God Himself did not make up these rules or these consequences. They are laws and principles that He too has had to live by while working out His own salvation (*Teachings of the Prophet Joseph Smith,* 345). Does this change your feelings toward God? Does it soften your heart toward Him?

1.7 Alma 32:6—Afflictions…humbled them…in a preparation to hear the word.

Here is another glimpse of God's purpose in allowing us to be afflicted by insurmountable experiences. It is to get our attention, to pull us back from the distractions of this world. It brings us to ourself, brings us to a consciousness of what is true. God allows all this to prepare us to hear "the word" that will lead us to know the Word, even Jesus Christ. Christ wants us to recover and to be at one with Him and with our Father who sent Him.

Application:

As you come to the end of this week's study of Step One and the principle of powerlessness, prayerfully summarize your thoughts concerning "powerlessness," "nothingness," and "humility." Realizing that "few people will sincerely try to [embrace and internalize these principles] unless they have hit bottom" (*12&12*, 24), describe how this week's study has increased your willingness to define the place in which you now are as your "bottom."

Is your current level of addiction sufficiently deep enough and hard enough to be the firm bedrock from which to rebound, repent, and recover a spiritually believing, trusting life?

Step One: Week Two

2.1 Helaman 4:13—And because of...their boastings in their own strength, they were left in their own strength; therefore they did not prosper, but were afflicted and smitten.

The Lord is so agency oriented that He'll give us only as much strength as we are willing to acknowledge that we need. If we are determined to live by self-sufficiency and a standard of "I must do it myself" or "I *will* do it myself," He'll let us—even if, like the two-year-old who insists on tying his own shoes, we are a little premature in our estimation of our own ability.

Like the wise parent of that two-year-old, the Lord lets us keep trying until we finally are willing to submit ourselves to Him and let Him guide our hands, our hearts, and our minds. While it is true that **"this life is the time for men to prepare to meet** [i.e. be like] **God" (Alma 34:32)**, He never intended that we do that learning and preparing alone, without His constant counsel (see **Alma 37:37**).

Application:

The common way to define those days when we do not participate in our addictive or compulsive behavior is in terms of abstinence—in other words, in terms of our ability to abstain.

Ponder and prayerfully write about what it would mean to our humility if we thought in terms of days of *deliverance*, rather than days of abstinence. How would this shift in focus from abstinence to deliverance help us to avoid boasting of our own strength?

2.2 Mosiah 29:19—They must unavoidably remain in bondage until now.

There is no way we can avoid, by ourselves, the bondage of our addiction. "No amount of human willpower [can] break it" (*12&12*, 22).

Our will *must* be connected to God's power if we are ever to be free.

Application:

Ponder and prayerfully write about your experience at exerting willpower to overcome your weakness. Was willpower ever enough to completely overcome the challenge? It may seem to work for awhile, but then what happens?

Do you know someone who seems to have tremendous willpower? They make up their mind and they do it—whatever it is—never looking to the left, or to the right, or to the heavens. Are you, or were you, ever like that?

Write about what is missing from this approach to recovery. What might these people still have to learn?

2.3 2 Nephi 9:42—And save they shall...consider themselves fools before God, and come down in the depths of humility, he will not open unto them.

By the time addiction has had its way with us, most of us have come to a place of "pitiful and incomprehensible demoralization" (*AA*, 30). We don't want to try again, just to end up a failure, looking like a fool. We come to a place of complete defeat, of "absolute humiliation" (*12&12,* 21).

At this point, we have nothing left with which to bargain with the Lord. We are in a state of total surrender. It is from this state of surrender that we are able to seek Him with a broken heart and a contrite spirit. It is then, and only then, that He can fully come to us.

> Our human resources [within ourselves and others], as marshaled by the will, were not sufficient; [sooner or later] they failed utterly (*AA*, 45).

Application:

This verse speaks of those who are prone to put more faith in the learning, wisdom, and riches of the world than in God. Ponder and prayerfully write about how many arm-of-flesh psychological or physical cures you've tried. How many, if any, gave more than a passing mention to the spiritual life?

A Twelve Step program of recovery defines Step One as a crisis of the most life-changing proportions. It challenges us to "face the proposition that either God is everything or else He is nothing. God either is, or He isn't. What [is] our choice to be?" (*AA*, 53).

Write about your readiness to make this choice, and what that choice will be.

Consider the following:

> The spiritual life is not a theory. *We have to live it* (*AA*, 83).

How do you feel about living life from the inside out? Has living from the outside in brought much genuine peace or happiness? (Read "Born of God," Ezra Taft Benson, *Ensign*, July 1989, 4.)

2.4 Alma 15:5—And they went in unto the house unto Zeezrom; and they found him upon his bed, sick, being very low with a burning fever; and his mind also was exceedingly sore because of his iniquities; and when he saw them he stretched forth his hand, and besought them that they would heal him.

Zeezrom was powerless to help himself. He could not free himself from the pain of his iniquities, which manifested in the form of physical illness. Many illnesses presented to medical doctors for treatment are caused or aggravated by mental or emotional stress. Only God can still these tempests within.

To get the most from your participation in a Twelve Step program of recovery, you have to admit that "...you may be suffering from an illness which only a spiritual experience will conquer" (*AA*, 44).

Application:

Ponder and prayerfully write about any physical ailments that you suspect, or outright *know*, were magnified and/or caused by the same fears and inner turmoil that drove you to your addiction.

Have you found yourself caught in a terrible spiral of various illnesses brought on by your addiction? Describe how this spiral has manifested itself in your life.

2.5 Alma 13:28—That ye may not be tempted above that which ye can bear.

Before taking Step One, we may find that we put ourselves in the way of temptation. We experiment with "countless vain attempts to prove" we can behave like a non-addicted person in relationship to our addictive behavior (*AA*, 30). It is only God's power that relieves us of this "insane urge" to continue to "ultimately destroy ourselves" (*12&12*, 22).

Application:

Ponder, remember, and prayerfully write about some of the times in the past when you have played with fire, trying to prove that this time you could handle it, that you could stop whenever you wanted. Alcoholics Anonymous compares this to a person with an insane compulsion to jaywalk in front of traffic—the bigger and the faster the vehicle, the better. Over and over he gets hit and put in the hospital, only to get out and try it again (see *AA*, 37–38).

One of the signs of an addiction is that, while you might be very functional and sane in every other area of your life, in this area you have no lasting control. Write about whether you're really ready to give up that pretense of control over your addiction.

2.6 Alma 22:14—[Man] could not merit *anything of himself* (emphasis added).

Sometimes we think that self-knowledge, gained from psychology and medical science, will cure us of our need to use our addictive behavior. However, true addicts soon learn that this is not so:

> [Someone who is truly addicted] will be *absolutely unable to stop... on the basis of self-knowledge.* This is a point we wish to emphasize and re-emphasize... (*AA,* 39).

We are all part of the fallen condition of man. We cannot merit anything of ourselves. Our situation is hopeless without the Savior. It is not through a relationship with alcohol, or excess food, or illicit sex, or overworking, or overspending—but through a relationship with our Savior that we can be restored to **"a perfect brightness of hope" (2 Nephi 31:20).**

How crazy is it, then, that in our pride and rebelliousness, we keep trying to bring about our own recovery through "every form of self-deception and experimentation," even using our outward behavior as active members of the Church to "prove [ourselves] exceptions to the rule?" (*AA,* 31).

Application:

Ponder and prayerfully write about self-knowledge. To what lengths have you gone, what kind of money have you spent, seeking to know yourself or to find yourself?

Joseph Smith made the statement, "If men do not comprehend the character of God, they do not comprehend themselves" (*Teachings of the Prophet Joseph Smith,* 343). What does this imply about the importance of coming to God and learning to know Him? How does knowing God have an impact upon knowing yourself?

2.7 Ether 3:2—We are unworthy before thee; because of the fall our natures have become evil continually.

To *be evil* is most broadly and yet most precisely defined as *being separated from God*. Thus, because of the fall we are all separated from God—at least in the physical sense. Remembering this helps us to realize why the brother of Jared would make such an inclusive statement. His statement takes in all of us, even the most feverishly active saint.

We are all *continually* separated from God while in this physical realm of life, and we must all learn to rely completely upon the spiritual realm and to develop a spiritual life.

Application:

Ponder and prayerfully write about what it means to be unworthy and in a state of "evil continually." Can you do anything about the fall or about your own fallen nature?

Sometimes we wonder how we got ourselves into such **"a dark and dreary waste,"** as our life seems to be at times. Paradoxical as the answer may be, Lehi's dream can be likened unto each of us. Read and ponder **1 Nephi 8: 5–7.** Who is the man in the white robe? How is it that we apparently followed Him in entering mortality, *and* that it is only by following Him that we can be led out of the effects of the fall?

Step One—Week Three

3.1 Mormon 2:26—Nevertheless the strength of the Lord was not with us; yea, we were left to ourselves, that the Spirit of the Lord did not abide in us.

Before learning about the Twelve Steps and recovery, I would read the Book of Mormon and be so perplexed and put off by all the accounts of wars and bloodshed. Then came the day I realized the whole book is about the absolutely universal natural-man tendency to turn away from God and try to live life without Him.

I have come to realize that God *never* initiates a separation between us. If He has left me to myself, it is because I have already, however subtly, started looking to my addiction to provide what only God can supply—the strength to stand against my life's challenges (enemies).

Application:

Write a history of your relationship with the Book of Mormon. When, and at what ages, and to what effect have you read it in the past? Has your reading always been for the purpose of completing an assignment, or a goal of quantity? How are these questions helping you to focus more upon quality?

3.2 Mormon 5:23—Know ye not that ye are in the hands of God? Know ye not that he hath all power?

This verse rehearses again, in harmony with **Mosiah 4:9,** the stark fact that God has all power—not just part, not just some—but *all*.

> Lack of power, that was our dilemma. We had to find a power by which we could live, and it had to be a *Power greater than ourselves*. Obviously. But where and how were we to find this Power?
>
> Well, that's exactly what this book is about. Its main object is to enable you to find a Power greater than yourself which will solve your problem.... And [that] means, of course, that we are going to talk about God (*AA*, 45).

Application:

If all power in heaven and on earth is really God's power, where is the power you are using—even at this moment to breathe and to read these words—coming from? When we think of willpower, to whom do we usually give the credit for whatever gets accomplished—self or God?

Prayerfully write about the idea that even though all power is God's, He honors the supreme principle of agency and allows us to use it according to *our own will* (see **Alma 29:4**).

3.3 Alma 38:14—Acknowledge your unworthiness before God at all times.

Alma reminds his son, Shiblon, to be **"not lifted up unto pride" (Alma 38:11).**

And again, he advises him, **"Do not say: O God, I thank thee that we are better than our brethren; but rather say: O Lord, forgive my unworthiness" (Alma 38:14).**

Often we disguise our powerlessness in a very strange way. We say, in effect, "Oh, I would have plenty of power to do what I want if it just weren't for__________" and then we fill in the blank with the name of a person, or the description of a set of circumstances, or an event that we blame for our poor choice(s).

Application:

Ponder and prayerfully write about your excuses—the other people and events that you've used to explain why you couldn't make a right choice; why you had to make a poor choice; why you had to use your addiction. Think of at least one specific incident and write a short narrative or story about it.

3.4 Helaman 13:6—And *nothing* can save this people save it be repentance (emphasis added).

Nothing can save this people unless they repent, or in other words, return to God. Why? Because without

God we are nothing. We are helpless and pitifully adrift on the raging sea of mortality.

Application:

Ponder and prayerfully write about how listening to the evening news can make you feel as if you're adrift on the raging sea of mortality.

Now look closer to home. How do the events or choices made in the lives of your family members make you feel? What about events or choices in your own life? Does self-pity help you deal with these realities, or does it make it worse? How does self-pity stop you from seeking God?

3.5 Moroni 9:22—For I know that they must perish *except they repent and return unto him* (emphasis added).

It's interesting that this verse is worded so that repenting and turning unto God are mentioned in sequence. It teases out the truth that many people do the one, but not the other. Many people picture repenting as stopping the detrimental behavior. They do not realize that repenting also includes turning to God.

To repent does not mean to turn *away*, but rather to turn *to*. Sometimes we try to turn to something else—like service to others, or a worthwhile hobby or interest. We usually find that these things are good *as far as they go*—but they don't go far enough. Only returning to God has the power we need.

Application:

Ponder and prayerfully write about the many times you have tried to repent by turning away from your addictive behavior or other weaknesses. How have you tried to fill your time and attention in service to others, or in another worthwhile project? Have these activities helped? For how long?

3.6 Helaman 6:5—Unto the bringing down many of them into the depths of humility, to be the humble followers of God and the Lamb.

There are many who are followers of God and the Lamb in name, but not nearly so many who are *humble* followers. This was certainly true of me for the first twenty years I was a member of the Church. This brings to mind the Savior's own words:

> **Not every one that saith unto me, Lord, Lord, shall enter into the kingdom of heaven; but he that doeth the will of my Father who is in heaven (3 Nephi 14:21).**

Application:

Ponder this idea of being a follower of Christ—not just in name only, but in deep humility.

How do you feel this applies to your membership in the Church? Has your membership in His Church been in name only? Or do you feel you have truly come to know Him personally?

If you were a disciple of Christ during His earthly ministry, how close to Him would you try to position yourself? Would you seek to sit at His knee, trusting His acceptance and love for you, or would you hang back, sitting at a distance?

3.7 Alma 37:33—Preach unto them repentance, and faith on the Lord Jesus Christ; teach them to humble themselves and to be meek and lowly in heart; teach them to withstand *every* temptation of the devil, with their faith on the Lord Jesus Christ (emphasis added).

We can only withstand *every* temptation when our faith is firmly planted upon the Lord Jesus Christ. Faith in any other source of strength or comfort will eventually fail us.

Grace is the enabling power of Jesus Christ that gives us the "strength and assistance" to *maintain* good works (see Bible Dictionary, "Grace," 697, emphasis added). We, by ourselves, are great at starting good works, but it is only through He who has answered **"the ends of the law"** that we can maintain these good works **"unto perfection"** (see **2 Nephi 2:7**).

Application:

Find "grace" in the Bible Dictionary and underline the phrases "enabling power" and "strength and assistance" to "maintain" a good work.

Christ is often called **"the author and the finisher of our faith" (Moroni 6:4).** In fact, we are taught that true discipleship exists only for those who know that they are **"relying alone upon the merits of Christ" (Moroni 6:4).**

Ponder and prayerfully write about grace as an enabling power. What does the word "alone" in the preceding phrase convey to your mind? Do we have any merits that we can rely on?

Step One—Week Four

4.1 Enos 1:4—And my *soul* hungered (emphasis added).

The spirit and the body are both components of the soul. It's obvious to all of us that it is possible for the body to hunger and thirst, and even to crave some certain substance if it has become dependent upon that substance for chemical functioning.

The spirit hungers and thirsts, too. It hungers and thirsts for that state of peace and surety that it knew in the premortal life, while in the presence of God. It hungers for the sense of being at one with God and with all creation. It hungers and thirsts for a restoration, or *recovery*, of that state of existence.

This is the deepest application of the concept of recovery: to be recovered by the Spirit and presence of God; to be able to discern His influence in your own heart and mind. This is a state of being that we are absolutely powerless to create on our own. It is also a state of being for which there is no substitute in the things of this world.

Application:

Ponder and prayerfully write your thoughts and feelings concerning *recovery*. What level of recovery do you honestly desire to attain at this point in your journey? Recovery of sobriety? Of a healthy body weight? What about recovery of financial solvency? Recovery of healthy, wholesome sexual relations with your spouse? What is it that is missing in your life that your soul hungers for? Do you long for (crave) to be returned to the presence of God?

You can attain that state of existence your soul hungers for, *even while mortal*. Read **Moroni 7:3** and write about the meaning of the phrase, **"from this time henceforth."** According to this verse, when are we promised to be rescued from our frantic need for our addictions?

4.2 2 Nephi 4:18—I am encompassed about, because of the temptations and the sins which do *so easily beset me* (emphasis added).

> Step One showed us an amazing paradox: We found that we were totally unable to be rid of the [addictive tendency] until we first admitted that we were powerless over it. (*12&12*, 107)

Some people really balk at the idea of admitting they are powerless, overwhelmed, undone. There are also people who object to the practice of stating that they are an alcoholic, or an addict, or a compulsive eater, or any other label of addiction.

These people do not understand that this admission of powerlessness—which sounds like defeat—is really ground zero. It's the place from which everything in our lives can launch off in a new and wonderful direction. Until we come to this point, we are trudging aimlessly around in the wilderness of self-sufficiency, self-will, self-rightness, and self-pity.

Application:

Read the Psalm of Nephi in its entirety **(2 Nephi 4:16–35)**. These verses are such a beautiful expression of our mortal circumstances. Ponder and prayerfully write your feelings of being **"encompassed about"** by your problems or addictions.

How have you tried to save yourself, to be victorious over your addictions—only to find yourself, once again, **"droop[ing] in sin?" (v. 28)**.

4.3 Moroni 9:18—Behold, I am but a man, and I have but the strength of a man, and I cannot...enforce my commands.

In these words, we find Mormon admitting the same truth that Alma admits in **Alma 29:3**. Like both of them, we are also **"but a man,"** or in other words, but mortal people.

No matter how righteous our desires, our commands to ourselves, or the wishes of our hearts, *we cannot bring our desires, commands, or wishes to pass.* Unlike Alma, we resist accepting this truth. We refuse to be satisfied with things as they are. We turn to our addictions, trying to make our world fit our desires.

Sometimes, in fact, we turn to our addictions because we feel it is the only thing we can control, the only thing we can have our way. We tell ourselves we can control it. Unfortunately, all too soon, it ends up controlling us.

Once we admit we are powerless, we can let go of the lie that tells us we can accomplish the things we wish, desire, or try to command. Only then are we finally in a position of humility where God can open His power and His guidance to us.

Application:

Ponder and prayerfully write about the frustration of wanting something to happen—something that from all outward appearances would seem to be for the best (wanting someone to love you; someone to learn to love God; to stop their course of self-destruction; to stop being abusive; wanting a better job for yourself; wanting a particular spouse; wanting to stay married).

Did those feelings of frustration trigger your desire to use your addiction? Do they still?

Write about what it means to let go and to let God be in charge of it all—to let God decide when, or if, your wishes or desires will be fulfilled.

4.4 Alma 26:12—I know that I am *nothing*; as to my strength I am weak (emphasis added).

This requires no comment. This truth is as plain and sharp as a surgical blade.

Application:

Read the verse in the context of **Alma 26:11–16**. It is part of a beautiful statement by Ammon about whose power brings him the success he was desiring.

Ponder and prayerfully write about the meaning of being *nothing*. When used in relationship to others, that word is a negative and abusive thing to say; when used in relationship to our total, absolute need for God, it becomes a wonderful, freeing experience.

4.5 Ether 12:27—And if men come unto me I will show unto them their weakness…for if they humble themselves before me, and have faith in me, then will I make weak things become strong unto them.

There are so many people, in and out of the Church, who absolutely go ballistic at the thought of us confessing our weaknesses. They insist that, even in private, we should do nothing but chant positive affirmations and give no attention to our weaknesses.

It is absolutely true that it does us no good to dwell, ruminate about, recycle, or rehash our weaknesses without taking them to Christ. However, *just the opposite is true* if we are looking at and baring our weaknesses in order to bring them to Christ.

Admitting our weaknesses and becoming humble is truly the first step to the strength the Lord has waiting for us.

Application:

Ponder and prayerfully write a list of all the things that you are powerless over in your life. Don't limit this list to just your addictive or compulsive behaviors. Put *everything* down.

Now list the things that you are sovereign and have decisive power over. I would suggest that the only thing that we can put on this second list is our willingness to surrender and trust God. (More about this in Step Three.)

4.6 1 Nephi 16:5—And it came to pass that they did humble themselves before the Lord; insomuch that I had joy and great hopes of them, that they would walk in the paths of righteousness.

We are often taught that the first principle of the Gospel is **"faith in the Lord Jesus Christ" (Articles of Faith 1:1)**. Of late, I've come to realize that "faith in the Lord Jesus Christ" is the first principle of *conversion* to the Gospel of Christ. Before the principle of faith, however, there must be a **"desire to believe"** (see **Alma 32:26–34**).

Alma indicates that first, people must be humbled by their afflictions. That is the first baby step that leads to a desire to change, to believe we can be changed, or redeemed. When that desire is acted upon, we exercise faith—and eventually come to a sure knowledge.

Because life is an ongoing process, we have to repeat that sequence again and again. Humility is teachableness, and it is never outgrown. Being teachable means remaining in a state of mind that keeps us in a state of humility—a state of acknowledgment of our continual nothingness without God. Only through "utter [not temporary] defeat are we able to take our first steps toward liberation and strength" (*12&12*, 21).

Application:

Ponder and prayerfully write about this process of coming to know for sure. At what point in the process are you, right now? Still being humbled? Humbled enough? Desiring to change? Desiring to believe you could change? Willing to take some action—to exercise faith? Willing to experiment upon these words?

This is the process of taking Step One. Write about how much or how little you feel ready for taking that first step.

4.7 Alma 13:13—I would that ye should humble yourselves before God, and bring forth fruit meet for repentance, that ye may also enter into that rest.

Here is another reference to that "rest" which we discussed previously in **Moroni 7:3**. Once we have given up the fight to be right or to be self-powered, it is as if we ourselves become a seed.

A seed often seems to be a dead, lifeless thing when it is buried in the ground. But then, after such a humbling experience, the seed begins to change. Even while still underground, great and miraculous changes are occurring. Eventually—sometimes sooner, sometimes later—the humble little seed bears observable growth and then fruit.

That can happen to us—here, now, in this life. As the Savior said, We must lose our life (our own self-centered way of coping) in order to find His Life—a life centered in and led by Him (see **Matthew 10:39**). In Him, there is all power. With Him, nothing is impossible. (More about that in Step Two's references and comments.)

Application:

Ponder and prayerfully write about the phrase "fruit meet for repentance." That's an old-fashioned way of wording the thought, but I don't believe it means, "You bring forth fruit (on your own) to prove you've repented."

In the light of the principle of powerlessness and nothingness without God that we have just studied, I think it is more correct to interpret this phrase to mean that after you have humbled yourself before Him. As such, you will begin to see His power manifest itself in your life and bring forth fruit. That fruit will give you the assurance you need to enter into that rest of hope and peace, that can only come from knowing Him and His personal love for you.

Supplemental Scriptures for Step One

The following are additional scriptures which support Step One:

2 Nephi 12:11—The Lord *alone* shall be exalted in that day (emphasis added). The Lord *alone* will be exalted. Our lofty looks and haughtiness fail us as we realize that we owe *everything* to Him.

2 Nephi 28:7–9—There shall be many which shall say: Eat, drink, and be merry. This could just as easily have been worded, "Eat, drink, and be numb"—numb to all the types of lies these three verses enumerate.

2 Nephi 31:7—Know ye not that he was holy? But notwithstanding he being holy...according to the flesh he humbleth himself before the Father. Our perfect exemplar showed us the way to humility.

Mosiah 1:13—And *he* will no more preserve them by his matchless and marvelous power (emphasis added). Even as a **"highly favored people,"** it is *God's* power that preserves us, not our own.

Mosiah 2:21—If ye should serve him with all your whole souls yet ye would be *unprofitable* servants (emphasis added). God is always pouring His support and power into us, lending us our very breath. The most active member of the church (prophets included) is in just as much need of His redemptive power as the most notorious rebel.

Mosiah 2:24–25—Therefore, of *what* have ye to boast? (emphasis added). More of the same truth: *we* have *nothing* of which to boast. Even if we've lived a nearly perfect life, who do we have to thank for that? *God.* What do we have to boast about? *Nothing.* Only as we connect with Him are we able to do anything of true worth.

Mosiah 3:19—For the natural man is an enemy to God, and has been from the fall of Adam, and will be, forever and ever, unless... As a natural man (or woman) I, *personally,* am powerless over my own natural, mortal being. The remainder of this verse gives us the steps we need to take.

Mosiah 4:10—And again, believe that ye must repent of your sins and forsake them, and humble yourselves before God; and ask in sincerity of heart that he would forgive you; and now, if you believe all these things see that ye do them. King Benjamin gives us the whole process in a nutshell.

Mosiah 4:11—I would that ye should remember...your own nothingness, and his goodness and long-suffering towards you, unworthy creatures, and humble yourselves even in the depths of humility.

Mosiah 23:11—For I am *unworthy* to glory of *myself* (emphasis added). More of the same testimony, this time from Ammon.

Alma 4:6—The people of the church began to wax proud, because of their exceeding riches... and all manner of precious things, which they had obtained by their industry. Like the people of the church in Alma's day, we tend to wax proud and give ourselves the credit for our own industry.

Alma 4:15—Alma, having seen the afflictions of the humble followers of God, and the persecutions which were heaped upon them by the remainder of his people, and seeing all their inequality, began to be very sorrowful. Seeing persecution and inequality produces sorrow in all of us, but we, like Alma, can know that **"the Spirit of the Lord** [will] **not fail** [us]."

Alma 5:54—Yea, will ye persist in supposing that ye are better one than another? Many of us come to a Twelve Step program with the idea that we are either better than others, or much worse than anyone else. We may believe that we are terribly victimized or terribly guilty. In truth, each of us is neither better nor worse that any other individual, in the sense that we are all children of God. We are all here to be tested. The same principles of the Gospel pertain to all.

Alma 7:3—I have come having great hopes and much desire that I should find that ye had humbled yourselves before God, and that ye had continued in the supplicating of his grace, that I should find that ye were blameless before him. Continued supplication for His grace is the only true path to getting rid of the toxic blame and shame many of us are burdened with.

Alma 30:17—And many more such things did he say unto them, telling them that...every man fared in this life according to the *management* of the creature; therefore every man prospered according to *his genius,* and that every man conquered according to *his strength*

(emphasis added). These teachings reveal Korihor as an antichrist. Too often we insist that our success has (or can) come as a result of our own good management, genius, or strength. When we are ready to admit that our life is unmanageable, no matter how much we strive or do on our own, we have taken Step One.

Alma 32:8—I behold that ye are lowly in heart; and if so, blessed are ye. To be brought down into the depths of humility and to be made lowly in heart doesn't feel like much of a blessing while it is happening. However, it will bring us to the greatest blessing of all—ultimate recovery and eternal life.

Alma 32:25—For I do not mean that ye all of you have been compelled to humble yourselves; for I verily believe that there are some among you who would humble themselves, let them be in whatsoever circumstances they might. We always have our agency and the opportunity to choose to turn to God at any time. We may each be at different levels of unmanageability. What is important is the decision we make to admit our own powerlessness.

Alma 42:30—Let the justice of God, and his mercy, and his long-suffering have full sway in your heart; and let it bring you down to the dust in humility. Focusing on God, rather than self, and considering His constancy in justice, mercy, and long-suffering can bring us to the correct understanding of ourselves in relationship to Him.

Alma 48:20—And thus they [Helaman and his brethren] **went forth, and the people did *humble* themselves *because of their words*...and thus they were free from**

wars and contentions among themselves (emphasis added). We can be brought to this correct understanding of our relationship to God and our need for humility by heeding the words of His prophets, thus saving us from needing to be compelled.

Alma 51:21—Thus he put an end to the stubbornness and the pride of those people...but they were brought down to humble themselves like unto their brethren, and to fight valiantly for their freedom from bondage. Pride is the enemy we are valiantly fighting against. Freedom comes through submission to God. We must be willing to turn this sin of stubbornness and pride over to Him.

Alma 62:49—But notwithstanding their riches, or their strength, or their prosperity, they were not lifted up in the pride of their eyes; neither were they slow to remember the Lord their God; but they did *humble themselves exceedingly before him* (emphasis added). Humility prepares us to be taught and gives us the willingness to do God's will.

Helaman 12:7—O how great is the nothingness of the children of men. Can it be said any plainer?

3 Nephi 6:13—Some were lifted up in pride, and others were exceedingly humble; some did return railing for railing, while others would receive railing and persecution and all manner of afflictions, and would not turn and revile again, but were humble and penitent before God. There are two ways that we can choose to react to the persecutions and afflictions that occur in our own lives.

Mormon: Chapters 2–4. These chapters can be seen as a parable or metaphor for the struggle waged against our greatest enemies—our addictions and compulsions. As we read these chapters, we may think of them as symbolizing the manner in which we mortals insist upon relying upon our own strengths to win the battles in our lives.

Mormon 3:3—And they did not realize that it was the Lord that had spared them... Are we possessed of the same pride that possessed these people? Will we spend our lives refusing to acknowledge that it is the Lord who has spared us, preserved us, and upheld us? Or will we give the credit to Him, even when it looks like we have succeeded on our own?

Mormon 9:5—For behold, when ye shall be brought to see your nakedness before God... This verse reminds me of **Mosiah 4:19** in which King Benjamin nails the point: **"Are we not all beggars...?"** When are we going to realize that whatever we're clothed with—our positions, our possessions, our very bodies themselves—it is all given to us and sustained for us by God?

Mormon 9:26—Behold, all ye who are despisers of the works of the Lord, for ye shall wonder and perish. That's pretty strong language, **"despisers of the works of the Lord."** Unfortunately, most of us fit into that category in a subtle, but very real way. Almost without exception, when we try to give the Lord credit for something it appears we have done by our own industry or genius, we receive the reply: "But *He* couldn't have done it without *you*." Does the blasphemy in those words show up when it's written in black and white?

Ether 9:35—When they had humbled themselves sufficiently before the Lord he did send rain...And the Lord did show forth his *power* unto them in preserving them from famine (emphasis added). Another reminder of our *lack* of power compared to the Lord's. Yet, in our humility, He does deliver us.

Moroni 7:24—And all things which are good cometh of Christ; otherwise men were fallen, and there could no good thing come unto them. *All* good that has ever been done, anywhere in all the world, by any mortal (whether Christian, Buddhist, agnostic, or atheist) has come **"of Christ."** Without His light shed abroad among all men, even among those who do not acknowledge or accept Him, **"no good thing [would] come unto them."**

Moroni 7:44—For none is acceptable before God, save the meek and lowly in heart. To be **"meek and lowly in heart"** is to take pride in nothing. It is to gain absolutely *none* of our self-esteem from anything that we've done, or that we own. Simply, we esteem ourselves because we are *His* children.

Other References for Step One

As you find other references to Step One in your personal daily scripture study, list them here:

Step Two

Came to believe that a Power greater than ourselves could restore us to sanity. Came to believe that God has all power and all wisdom, and that in His strength we can do all things

Many Latter-day Saints who are new to the Twelve Steps read the words "came to believe" and minimize or tune out the second step entirely, thinking that belief in God is not a problem or an issue for them.

This is a disastrous action. We must be humble enough to realize we are not above any of the steps. We must be "willing to go to any length" to find recovery, even if it means following a pathway blazed by alcoholics (*AA*, 58). If our level of humility and open-mindedness is even one bit less than this, our efforts to recover will be defeated.

Step Two contains a principle that is as critical to our recovery and as challenging to the average LDS mindset as was the absolute humility required in Step One. Step Two is the principle of *grace*.

We avoid the idea of grace and esteem it almost as a falsity. possibly because of the stress placed on it in other Christian religions. Yet, grace is defined as an "enabling power," a "divine means of help or strength given through the bounteous mercy and love of Jesus Christ." This grace, or power, is absolutely necessary for a person to "do good works that they otherwise would not be able to maintain if left to their own means" (Bible Dictionary, "Grace," 697).

People struggling with compulsive addictive behaviors lack the power to maintain recovery or sanity. We are great at starting a new effort to stay sober, clean, abstinent, sane. Time after time we promise ourselves and others that we will never practice our addiction again. But without the enabling power of Christ, we cannot maintain our commitment. Sooner or later we "use" again.

Thus we and our loved ones are jerked around the degrading, destructive cycle of addiction again and again. Hopeless as our situation may seem, the simple act of being willing to believe is all that it takes to make a beginning. Alma stated it best when he said:

> **If ye can no more than desire to believe** [in Christ]**, let this desire work in you (Alma 32:27).**

Step Two also gives us access to the great attribute of hope. If we can "come to believe" that God has the power to restore us to sanity, we can cling to that shred of hope in our otherwise hopeless state. We can then watch our hope grow as our faith increases. Charity for ourselves and for others begins to blossom. As Moroni teaches us:

> **Wherefore, there must be faith; and if there must be faith there must also be hope; and if there must be hope there must also be charity (Moroni 10:20).**

Because of this extension of hope, Step Two becomes the rallying point for all who have admitted personal powerlessness and are reaching for a Power greater than themselves.

> Therefore, Step Two is the rallying point for all of us....True humility and an open mind can lead us to faith, and...assurance that God will restore us to sanity if we rightly relate ourselves to Him (*12&12*, 33).

Step Two—Week One

1.1 Moroni 7:38—No man can be saved...save they shall have faith...[in Christ, not in themselves. If this complete surrender to Christ is not attained, then] **awful is the state of man, for they are as though there had been no redemption made.**

> ...the one who says he won't believe... He is in a state of mind which can be described only as savage (*12&12*, 25; emphasis added).

Here we find a perfect description of the natural man in all his enmity towards God. This is the person who *won't* believe, who *wills* not to believe. This kind of person *chooses* not to believe. His disbelief is not because he is confused or overwhelmed with pain, but because he has resentment and bitterness toward God.

I am grateful to say that I have not come across many people who are this deliberately hateful towards God. Most of us, I believe out of ignorance of His great goodness and mercy, or fear of His judgment and wrath, resist the testimony that Christ can redeem all, even ourselves. We act as if God's desire is to punish and demote us, not to teach and exalt. We hold ourselves back from recovery by *pre*-judging ourselves. We will not *let* Him administer healing and peace to us.

As amazing as it may sound, God cannot save us without our consent. The truth is, our own judgment of ourselves is even more final than God's (see **Alma 29:4; D&C 88:32**). He may long to extend mercy and full recovery and redemption to us, but if we will not accept it—if we insist we are not yet ready, not yet worthy, that we haven't done "all that we can do"—then we remain separated from Him. We remain in a state of condemnation, not by God, but by ourselves. Simultaneously, we have condemned and rejected Him and His offer of atonement.

Application:

Ponder and prayerfully write about this idea of resisting the salvation of Christ. How have you postponed turning to God by judging yourself unworthy or unready? In which aspects of your life have you decided you haven't done *enough*, haven't done *all that you can do*?

What does resisting salvation look like in your life? Do you hold on to guilt after those with proper authority have assured you of forgiveness? Over which actions or behaviors are you holding on to guilt and shame? Are they big things or little things?

Is God *really* a Power greater than yourself? Is He really powerful enough to redeem and to repair your shortcomings? What are your feelings about His power to redeem everyone, *even you*, and to make all things right?

1.2 Mormon 5:16—Without the power of God in our lives, we are driven about as chaff before the wind.

Is there a better metaphor for powerlessness?

On page 28 of the 12&12, the text addresses "those who once had faith, but have lost it" or forsaken it. There are several reasons for the loss referenced here. Either they: (1) "drifted into indifference;" (2) fell into the lie of "self-sufficiency" and have "cut themselves off" from the peace and assurance of God's power and presence; (3) "have become prejudiced against religion," (often by judging others who fail to practice the religion perfectly); or (4) are former believers "who are downright defiant because God has failed to fulfill their demands."

Application:

Ponder and prayerfully write about a period of time in your life when you have been inactive in the Church because of one of these attitudes: indifference, self-sufficiency, prejudice or judgment against other active members, or in outright defiance because your life was not going the way you wanted.

If you have never been inactive, write about a time when you may have been active on the outside, keeping up appearances—but still harboring one or more of these feelings or attitudes in your secret inner thoughts and beliefs.

1.3 1 Nephi 7:12—The Lord is able to do all things... for the children of men, if...they exercise faith in him.

As far back as I can remember, I have always believed in God and that He could do all things—with *one* exception. I did not believe He could save *me*.

In fact, I was certain He couldn't. After all, I had prayed constantly for years to be relieved of my addiction, and to no lasting avail. I was like this alcoholic described below:

> He's sure he still believes in God, but suspects that God doesn't believe in him (*12&12*, 32).

What I didn't realize then was, while I wanted to stop my addictive behavior and its consequences, I wasn't willing to be changed *in my heart*. Now I know that God can only restore us to sanity if we are willing to believe He can. If we think we are greater than He, that we have more power to mess up than He has to redeem and recover, then we haven't yet come to believe in a power greater than ourselves.

Some of us are too terrified by the truth of our own powerlessness to give up believing that we're all-powerful. But give it up we must, or we will be unable to exercise faith in Him. It's as if our belief that we are all-powerful is using up the same energy or space which we must have in order to exercise faith in Him.

Application:

Ponder and prayerfully write about whether you really believe God has the power to save you. If you find you do believe He has that power, then you're ready to face the more likely hang-up: whether you believe He will save *you*. Explore and write about how you feel about whether He cares to save you, whether He will go to any lengths to save you.

Write a letter to your Heavenly Father, sharing your honest feelings. Be humble and believing. Listen for answering thoughts and impressions to come into your mind. Record this conversation with Him. He loves you. He *will* answer you with mercy and kindness. Remember, as the prophets themselves have testified, He would have died to save even one of us. He longs for you to let that one be you.

1.4 2 Nephi 24:3—The Lord shall give thee rest, from thy sorrow, and from thy fear, and from the hard bondage wherein thou wast made to serve.

When the earliest members of Alcoholics Anonymous sought medical and psychological help, they were told that they were "100% hopeless, apart from divine help" (*AA*, 43).

No truer words have ever been uttered about the **"hard bondage"** of addiction. Only the Lord can give you rest and recovery. Other sources may give you distraction from your pain, but only God will give you the peace which **"passeth all understanding" (Philippians 4:7)**. This feeling of peace, or rest, makes no sense, considering your outward circumstances. But there you are, at peace.

Our addictions may seem to give us a type of peace, but it is always temporary. The pain is not eliminated, just temporarily held at bay. Sooner or later we must face it. Only Christ can give us the kind of peace which prepares us for anything—facing our past (inventory in Step Four) or facing our future, free of the burden of lies we once believed and lived. Thus we must seek "His protection and care with complete abandon" (*AA*, 59).

Application:

Ponder and prayerfully write about what the words "complete abandon" mean to you. How much trust would it take to relate to the Lord with this kind of childlike faith and trust? How sane is it to keep reaching for something that only gives temporary relief? How ready are you to take the necessary steps to find the Lord's rest?

1.5 Ether 12:4—Whoso believeth in God might with surety hope for a better world,...which hope cometh of faith, maketh an anchor to the souls of men, which would make them sure and steadfast.

Coming to believe in God brings us hope, not only for ourselves, but for those around us. If we can believe that God is truly in charge, that "nothing, absolutely nothing happens in God's world by mistake" (*AA*, 449), we can have hope for our loved ones. We can accept (not condone) the evil we see in our world, knowing Jesus Christ and His atonement are powerful enough to overcome it. Christ is an anchor to our souls. In Him, our sanity is secure.

When I first read that quote, "Nothing happens in God's world by mistake," I was tempted to think, "Yeah, but that's the point—*this* isn't God's world. Satan rules here." Almost instantly, I felt the lie in that thought. This is *still* God's world. Everything which happens here, happens with His allowance. All of it, even the most painful and unfair parts, can be used for His own benevolent purposes. Suddenly, I could see that, in that sense, there are no mistakes. Eve didn't make a mistake. She was fulfilling Heavenly Father's purposes for this earthly experience.

In **Genesis 45:8**, this truth surfaces again in the scriptures. Joseph testifies to his brothers that it was not really their hand which sent him into Egypt, but God's. No mistake was made, not even in their unrighteous intentions or actions. God has the power to weave such choices into His own purposes. Even Satan's part is planned into God's world. In the final truth, we are never outside the will of God.

Application:

Ponder and prayerfully write about this idea of believing God when he instructs his prophet (King Benjamin) to declare:

> **Believe in God; believe that he is, and that he...** [has] **all power, both in heaven and in earth (Mosiah 4:9).**

Focus on the ideas of *all power* and *both in heaven and in earth*. Does this feel like an anchor to your soul? Does it help to know that ultimately God is in charge and that His purposes will be fulfilled, even through or despite your mistakes?

Make a list of some of the positive experiences you've had as a result of actions you thought were mistakes.

1.6 Helaman 14:13—Ye may have a remission of [your sins] through his merits.

Many addicts testify to the fact that it is only in and through God that they have found abstinence, or remission, from their addictions.

> My friend sat before me, and he made the point-blank declaration that God had done for him what he could not do for himself. His human will had failed. Doctors had pronounced him incurable. Society was about to lock him up. Like myself, he had admitted complete defeat. Then he had, in effect, been raised from the dead, suddenly taken from the scrap heap to a level of life better than the best he had ever known!...Here was something at work in a human heart which had done the impossible (*AA*, 11).

God can restore you to sanity. He can give you peace, remission of your sins, an end to your guilt and anger, to your grief and pain. Nothing else on earth can do that—not even your obsessive, compulsive efforts to change and be perfect. No amount of our own willpower will make us worthy or perfect. Our sins and guilt are **"swept away"** by His power, not whittled away by our merits (see **Enos 1:6**).

Application:

Ponder and prayerfully write a brief history of your attempts to atone for your own sins through willpower, or by collecting merits through good deeds. How has this been an act of attributing the power and honor to the wrong source?

Reflect on how your history supports the statement that "human will had failed." Underline or copy into your journal any of the phrases or words from the previous quote that speak to your experience. Write about why they are meaningful to you.

1.7 Mosiah 3:18—Men drink damnation to their own souls except they humble themselves and become as little children, and believe that salvation was, and is, and is to come, in and through the atoning blood of Christ, the Lord Omnipotent.

Drinking damnation to our souls is pretty literal for some addicts. For others, it's a metaphor. For all of us, however, it's a form of hell.

When I first read through the AA material, I realized it consisted of the testimonies of a bunch of hopeless alcoholics claiming salvation from their self-imposed hell. Many of them had literally lived a life of sin and damnation. I was gripped by a shocking thought: Maybe it was me, not God, who had been passing judgment on my weaknesses. Maybe He hadn't abandoned me, but rather, I was refusing to come to Him with my shame and helplessness. After all, these drunks had found mercy.

I soon realized I was acting like the "good son," watching the prodigal showered with mercy and compassion from a loving Father I had not been humble enough to approach (see **Luke 15**).

Application:

Ponder and prayerfully write about your struggle to humble yourself and become as a little child, to receive Christ as your *personal* Savior. Why do you think you've resisted this, when the scriptures testify of His love for you?

If you could write your best friend a letter—and that best friend was Jesus—what would you say? Many of our Latter-day Saint hymns are addressed to Christ in this way. Using them as an example, write a letter to Christ. Share your thoughts and feelings about His sacrifice for you. Express your doubts and fears. Then, be still and listen for the response of the Spirit. Write about His answer of assurance to you.

Step Two—Week Two

2.1 1 Nephi 17:51—And now, if the Lord has such great power...he [can] instruct me...

Over the years, I have certainly racked up a list of solutions to my problems. I've gone from pillar to post and back again. I tried some options over and over again, even though they never showed much in the way of success. I wasn't the only one.

> Some of the methods we have tried [to limit our drinking and deceive ourselves into thinking we were in control]: Drinking beer only, limiting the number of drinks, never drinking alone, never drinking in the morning, drinking only at home, never having it in the house, never drinking during business hours,...swearing off forever (with and without a solemn oath), taking more physical exercise, reading inspirational books,... we could increase the list ad infinitum (*AA*, 31).

Some of us have dealt with alcohol addiction and find these methods of controlling our drinking all too familiar. Many of us, dealing with other addictive behaviors, make similar lists. Mine often looked like this: Only eating whole wheat flour, limiting calories, never eating alone, no eating between meals, never eating out, not allowing any sugar in my house, never eating while watching TV, and so forth.

The problem with trying to control our addictive behaviors is not that they weren't good ideas. It's that they weren't *inspired* ideas. I didn't counsel with the Lord. I just got the idea and went plunging ahead, then failed and felt even more demoralized.

As I practiced Step Two, I began to see the Lord as my primary therapist, and I began to pray for His guidance. The methods I was to use began to fall into place, along with everything else in my life. I was led to the right books to read, the right people to talk to, the right diet to try. When I allowed the Lord to orchestrate and design my recovery, it began to work.

Application:

List the ways you've tried to overcome your negative behaviors—medical doctors, counselors or therapists, vitamins, supplements, books, etc. Put a check by those you've prayed about and felt a witness from the Lord to include in your recovery program.

Make a second list of the many channels the Lord has used to instruct you (family, friends, books, etc.).

2.2 1 Nephi 13:16—And the power *of the Lord* was with them (emphasis added).

The natural man in each of us resists believing in and living a spiritual life. We try all kinds of gimmicks or tricks—like those we listed in the last exercise—to improve ourselves, not realizing that:

> If a mere code of morals or a better philosophy of life were sufficient…[we] would have recovered long ago (*AA*, 44).

Gradually, life humbles us and, like the alcoholic, we begin to realize that these "half measures availed us nothing" (*AA*, 59). We come to believe that no reliance or dependence on anything other than the Lord will empower us to fulfill the righteous desires of our hearts.

Do we desire to abstain from a certain destructive behavior? Then we must have *His* power to do so. Nothing less will suffice.

Application:

Write about the single longest period of abstinence you've had from your addiction. What kept your abstinence going; what caused it to be a success? Did this abstinence end? If so, what caused it to fail? Was it a half-measure from the beginning or did something happen to diminish your commitment?

2.3 **1 Nephi 1:20**—When we come to believe, come to have faith in Christ, we tap into a source of power that can finally make us **"mighty even unto the power of deliverance."**

> If, when you honestly want to, you find you cannot quit entirely [resist returning to your destructive behavior], or if [once you have started] you have little control…, you are probably [addicted]. If that be the case,

> you may be suffering from an illness which only a spiritual experience will conquer (*AA*, 44).

Can you relate? Do you have a behavior over which you seem to have little or no control? If so, then you have a problem that nothing less than a deep spiritual conversion to Christ and a daily, *living* walk with Him in the Spirit will cure. Only He is mighty enough to deliver you.

Application:

Ponder and prayerfully write about those things you've been turning to in the past for deliverance from your need to face the truth. Write about how facing the truth can help you come to know *the* Truth.

2.4 Alma 15:8—If thou believest in the redemption of Christ thou canst be healed.

To be healed is the equivalent of being restored to sanity. Being restored to sanity is being restored to a way of thinking about life—and the events and people in your life—which is based on truth about your immediate circumstances, as well as the truth of eternal principles. If we are willing to listen, Christ can teach us the truth of all things through the power of the Holy Ghost **(Moroni 10:5)**.

These truths—honesty and a willingness to do whatever it takes—are a part of everyone's path to recovery from addiction.

> Rarely have we seen a person fail who has thoroughly followed our path [of rigorous honesty]. Those who do not recover are people who are [or seem to be]...constitutionally incapable of being honest with themselves... [If] you want what we have [long-term abstinence] and are willing to go to any length to get it [be honest in all your thoughts, words, and actions]—then you are ready to take certain steps (*AA*, 58).

Application:

Ponder and prayerfully write about the way dishonesty creates the insanity of addiction. How does being rigorously honest bring you closer to the Savior and to recovery?

2.5 2 Nephi 2:2—He shall consecrate thine afflictions for thy gain.

Some people truly believe that the only afflictions which God can, or will, consecrate to our gain are those afflictions we had no hand in bringing upon ourselves. I know I felt that way.

Somewhere in my childhood, I had been riveted with the thought: "Well, he made his own bed, let him lie in it." (Notice the word 'rivet' and remember **D&C 123:7**.) The Lord might turn injuries in which I was an innocent bystander into eventual blessings for me, but if I was even the slightest bit responsible, I was on my own. I could only expect God's deliverance from the afflictions I didn't face due to my own poor choices. If it was my mistake, then it was "to heck with her [me]!"

Then one day, I read **Mosiah 4:17–18**. (Please go read it right now.) Here God tells us (me) how merciful He feels towards even those who have brought misery upon themselves. I came to believe that no matter what the tapes in my head said, the God of the Book of Mormon, Jesus Christ, had the kindness and charity to weave even my ignorant, willful actions into a greater plan. As soon as we're ready to believe, He can and He will.

Application:

Ponder and prayerfully write about an incident, big or small, when you were in the midst of your season of poorest choices, and yet something happened which you can now recognize as the Lord blessing you despite those poor choices. Are you beginning to realize the extent of God's patience and mercy?

What about right now? Are these principles changing your perspective on life? Whether yes or no, write about where you are in relationship to this Step Two concept? Reflect. Wonder. Ponder. Argue for or against it. Learn what you really believe.

2.6 2 Nephi 19:2—People that walked in darkness have seen a great light.

At a gathering of Latter-day Saints using the Twelve Step model of recovery, a young man rehearsed his witness which I have heard countless people bear:

> I was in the midst of one of the worst periods of my addiction—gone on my sinful way of living. I turned on the TV, looking for some sleazy program, and found a program teaching of God *and was pierced through my heart with the knowledge I had to return to God.* In the midst of the pigsty, the repentance of the prodigal began.

In the midst of his lowest period. Not in a moment of sobriety, but *in the midst of his addiction*. That is when the prodigal "came to himself." And so it is for many.

Bill Wilson's story, so similar to those of Paul and Alma the Younger, illustrates this principle. An abbreviated account of his story is found in *Alcoholics Anonymous*, pgs 13–14. From a more explicit account, he writes of this electric moment:

> Suddenly, my room blazed with an indescribably white light. I was seized with an ecstasy beyond description. Every joy I had known was pale by comparison. The light, the ecstasy—I was conscious of nothing else for a time.…Then came the blazing thought, 'You are a free man.'…I became acutely conscious of a Presence which seemed like a veritable sea of living spirit. I lay on the shores of a new world.…I knew that I was loved and could love in return. I thank my God, who had given me a glimpse of His absolute self (*Pass It On: The Story of Bill Wilson and How the A.A. Message Reached the World*, 121).

What is this great light spoken of by so many in recovery? It is the Light that was not afraid of lepers or harlots, of money changers or egotistical, self-righteous bigots like Saul. It is the Light of Christ. He will walk into any dark place to find us—whether it be darkness of environment or of heart. If there is even the tiniest ember of desire left in us, He *can* and He *will* restore us.

Application:

Ponder and prayerfully write about this idea of God's light being strong enough and merciful enough to find a person even in their darkest moment. How do you relate to this idea? Is it new to you or have you had a similar experience?

Write an account of a time when you were in the pits of deepest discouragement, despair, depression—and how, by studying these materials, you have gotten from there to here.

2.7 Alma 5:48—I know that Jesus Christ shall come… And behold, it is he that cometh to take away the sins of the world, yea, the sins of every man who steadfastly believeth on his name.

Jesus Christ can restore us to sanity (serenity) by taking away both the sins perpetrated against us *and* the sins that we ourselves have committed. When we accept the Atonement for the sins of others, we are released from the burden of blame and resentment. When we accept the Atonement for ourselves, we are freed from the hell of shame and self-loathing.

Application:

Ponder and write about the double-edged sword of resisting the Savior's atoning power to restore us to sanity. When we let Him into our hearts, holding nothing back, He frees us.

What feelings of resentment or shame do you carry in your heart? What would life be like without them? What reason would you have for wanting to continue to carry them? Wouldn't doing so be the equivalent of insanity?

Step Two—Week Three

3.1 **2 Nephi 2:6—Wherefore, *redemption* cometh in and through the Holy Messiah; for he is full of grace and truth (emphasis added).**

There are three "R's" which come to us through the power of working the Twelve Steps. Not only are we led through the steps of *repentance*, but we are also led to *recovery* and *redemption* through practicing and internalizing these true principles.

There is so much more than simple abstinence from our addiction awaiting us if we are willing to "keep coming back." We can, like Enos, feel a witness from God that our sins are not only forsaken by us—they are literally taken from us. Like Enos, we will also come to know that **"God could not lie" (Enos 1: 6)**.

Application:

In D&C 93:26, Christ declares Himself "the Spirit of truth," who has received "a fullness of truth, yea, even of all truth." As we take Step Two, we begin the process of seeking to live in a "fullness" of truth in our own lives and to repent of lying in any form, including pretending everything is okay when it really isn't.

Ponder and prayerfully write about your relationship to pretense—pretending something is true, when it really isn't. Make an inventory of the different seasons of your life and how honest you were able to be in each one: grade school, junior high, high school, young adult, etc. If you had to give up pretending in order to get sobriety, would you be willing to do so? Why or why not?

3.2 Ether 12:27—My grace is sufficient for all men that humble themselves before me; for if they humble themselves before me, and have faith in me, then will I make weak things become strong unto them.

In these words is found one of the most beautiful explanations of the way Step Two—having faith in God—endows us with the enabling power of Jesus Christ.

Application:

Here is another verse about grace. Do you remember how the LDS Bible Dictionary defines grace? Look it up again and underline some key phrases that stand out to your mind.

Note that grace is power to *maintain* a good work. How can grace help maintain abstinence? Capture and reflect on this and on any other phrases which cause you to want the application of His grace in your life.

3.3 2 Nephi 31:19—Relying wholly upon the merits of *him who is mighty to save* (emphasis added).

Christ is the only One who is truly *mighty to save*. He is the "power greater than ourselves" who can and will "restore us to sanity," just as soon as we are willing to have Him do so (see **Alma 29:4, "according to their wills"**).

So what is the answer to our dilemma of not being able to access the peace of the Atonement?

> The answer has to do with the quality of faith rather than its quantity (*12&12*, 32).

The *quality* of a person's faith, whether they are Latter-day Saints or of another faith, is based on one criterion only and can be assessed by one simple question: *What is your relationship with Jesus Christ?*

This question is a more personalized version of **"What think ye of Christ?" (Matthew 22:42)**. Do you know what it feels like to be in His presence, to feel of *His* spirit, to know you have been in the presence of Jesus Christ?

People describe variations of experiences with His spirit—the great wind, the bright light, a feeling of power and energy, a feeling of connectedness with all of the universe. His is the Spirit which testifies to you of truth—even the tiniest, work-a-day truths.

The Holy Ghost is the *mediator* for the words of Christ, but it is actually *Christ's* own counsel which you are receiving. It is He, through the miracle of the Holy Ghost's administration, who is your constant companion.

Application:

Ponder and prayerfully write about what you feel the greatest gift of the Holy Ghost could be. Think about the fact that the Holy Ghost conveys "the words of Christ." Could there be any greater gift?

The light of Christ, or conscience, has been compared to a receiving device built into us from before birth, which allows us to be in conscious contact with the Savior any time we need to be. How does this metaphor open your understanding of the Savior's power and love for each of us? How does it change things to know we can access His Spirit and His counsel through this device any time we're believing enough to do so?

3.4 Alma 5:12—And according to his faith there was a mighty change wrought in his heart.

This "mighty change wrought in [the] heart" is the equivalent of an "entire psychic change" (*AA*, p.xxix). It is a process which begins with our faith *in Christ* and continues through His power in us.

A complete psychic change is a pretty amazing thing. Your whole outlook on life is turned around; everything is defined differently. Where once you saw things as tragedies, you now define them as painful but powerful growing experiences. This psychic change begins when you accept the fact that there is a Power greater than yourself watching over and weaving all your life experiences together—*and that His intent is benevolent.*

Application:

Ponder and prayerfully capture from **Alma 5:12**. Write about your desire and willingness to have your whole paradigm, or model of life, changed from the inside (your heart) out.

Can you trust God with your most long-standing and entrenched fears and negative beliefs? Are you ready to give away the lies at the root of your negative beliefs? Why or why not?

3.5 Alma 25:6—For many of them, after having suffered much loss and so many afflictions,...began to disbelieve the traditions of their fathers, and to believe in the Lord, and that he gave great power.

Many of us are held back from believing in the Lord by the disbelieving traditions of our parents. In **D&C 123:7**, there is a powerful reference to the creeds of the parents, *who have inherited lies themselves,* which are riveted upon the hearts of the children. Only the Lord Jesus Christ has the power to remove rivets that strong.

Consider the traditions (beliefs, creeds) of your parents. What did they believe to be the proper relationship with God? Was it formal and distant? Was it close and intimate?

How about their beliefs about man/woman and husband/wife relationships? Was there a tradition of open, friendly communication? Was it of closeness or of distance? Was it one of mutual respect and admiration or was it competitive and adversarial?

What was their tradition relating to scripture? Total ignorance? Sunday only use? Daily study? Pondering and internalizing?

All of these traditions are expressions of your parents' beliefs or, to be more explicit and pointed, what they worship.

> We found, too, that we had been worshippers… Had we not variously worshipped people, sentiment, things, money, and ourselves? (*AA*, 54).

We naturally worship those things we think will bring us sanity and serenity. If our parents had righteous traditions, we learned to worship and rely on God. If our parents held false traditions, we learned to worship the false gods which led us to addiction.

Application:

Write about the traditions (beliefs, creeds) of your parents concerning the power of other things (such as education, social status, wealth, hard work, etc.) to bring happiness.

Do you hold to those beliefs or have you begun to disbelieve those traditions? Where do you now believe the power to bring happiness and peace resides?

3.6 Ether 6:3—And thus the Lord caused stones to shine in darkness.

All of us have done some pretty sad things—or had some pretty sad things done to us. These sad things sit in our hearts like rocks in our pockets, keeping our spirit from rising, preventing us from feeling joy, hope, gratitude, even whole-hearted love.

We have no power to change this on our own—no more than the Brother of Jared had power to transform stones into shining lights. But the Lord *does* have the power.

If we believe in His power to transform—to heal, to cause leprosy to disappear, to cause the dead to live again, and to make stones shine—He will touch the sad things in our hearts and transform them also. When His truth and His spirit are through, we will be able to look back at our past and see that our "stones" now shine and give off light to bless us and guide our future choices.

Application:

Ponder and prayerfully write about this metaphor of turning stones to shining lights and turning sad experiences into blessings. Another metaphor is that of turning of stumbling blocks into stepping stones.

Write about your belief in Christ. Take a good look at whether you really do believe He can heal leprosy, raise the dead, make ugly, gray rocks shine like diamonds with fire in them. Can you imagine that He could make you and all of your life experiences shine from the inside out?

3.7 Ether 12:8—And prepared a way that thereby others might be partakers of the heavenly gift.

There is no gift that is more heavenly, both figuratively and literally, than the gift of sanity which comes when you have been touched by the Spirit of God.

When Bill Wilson had his original spiritual experience which changed him so deeply and so profoundly that he lost all desire for alcohol, he was at first ecstatic, then frightened. He thought maybe he was switching insanities—from alcoholism to hallucinations. He hurriedly called the psychiatrist caring for him. After the doctor came and listened to Bill's account of his experience, his professional pronouncement was:

> "Something has happened to you. I don't understand what. But you had better hang

> on to it." ...The good doctor now sees many men who have such experiences. He knows that they are real (*AA*, 14).

In **Ether 12:6–8**, Moroni reminds us that we have to go through a trial of faith before God will reveal Himself to us—in Spirit, in voice, or in vision—whether quickly, as with Bill, Paul and Alma the Younger, or more slowly through an educational process which brings a gradual awakening.

Application:

Ponder and prayerfully write about the idea that a spiritual experience—whether gained instantly or gradually— changes us on an inner level. This inner change leads to outward changes in our behavior, our looks, our very lives.

In **Moses 3:5–7** and **Doctrine & Covenants 29:34**, we learn that the spiritual creation comes first. Write about your willingness to partake of just such a heavenly gift in order to have the external changes follow? Are you patient enough to work from the inside out?

Step Two—Week Four

4.1 1 Nephi 3:7—I know that the Lord giveth no commandments...save he shall prepare a way for them that they may accomplish [it]**.**

This verse is often quoted to emphasize Nephi's willingness to obey the Lord, but do we ever notice the reason for his willingness? We must look to God not only for direction, but for the power to follow that direction.

I can't tell you how many times I've heard this verse quoted over the years. Hundreds, maybe even thousands. But I never really heard the last part of the statement.

Why was Nephi willing to do what the Lord asked of him? Because he believed – he knew – that the Lord had the power to open the way for him to accomplish it. Those who have practiced Step Two come to know this simple fact, too.

> In fact, we could will these things [to be moral and sober] with all our might, but the needed power wasn't there. Our human resources, as marshaled by the will, were not sufficient; they failed utterly.
>
> Lack of power, that was our dilemma. We had to find a power by which we could live, and it had to be *a Power greater than ourselves* (*AA*, 45; italics original).

Application:

Ponder and prayerfully write about this dilemma, this lack of power. What human resources have you tried to marshal at different times in your life? Has willpower ever been sufficient? Why do you think that willpower is not enough to conquer addiction?

4.2 Mosiah 5:2—We know...[He] **wrought a mighty change in us, or in our hearts, that we have no more disposition to do evil, but to do good continually.**

Wow! This has got to be the ultimate Step Two scripture in the entire Book of Mormon. First of all, notice that *He*—"the Spirit of the Lord Omnipotent"—wrought the mighty change in them. They didn't do it themselves. They *couldn't* do it themselves. Only God could!

Go back to Step Two, "Came to believe that a Power greater than ourselves could restore us to sanity." Pay attention to that capital "P." That "P" isn't referring to your Twelve Step friends, your group, your sponsor, your therapist, your own writing or study. That capital "P" is reserved for Divinity—for God. The power to change our hearts is vested in the Son, Jesus Christ, by our caring, loving Heavenly Father and transmitted to our spirits and to our minds by the administration of the Holy Ghost. All three members of the Godhead are absolutely essential to the process of redemption and recovery.

"No more disposition to do evil." This isn't just about changing our outward behavior. This is about changing our inward thoughts and feelings, our inclinations and beliefs. This is heart-deep change.

Application:

Ponder and prayerfully write about this "Power greater than ourselves." Have you experienced this power in your life?

Include your reflections on heart-deep change as contrasted and compared with outward changes in behavior. Can we have one without the other? Which causes the other? How often have you tried to change from the outside-in? What have been the results? Is there any good in changing behavior first? What danger lies in focusing only on changing our outward behavior?

4.3 2 Nephi 25:26—And we talk of Christ, we rejoice in Christ, we preach of Christ, we prophesy of Christ, and we write according to our prophecies, that our children may know to what source they may look for a remission of their sins.

This same concept exists in *Alcoholics Anonymous,* also called the *AA Big Book*. Those who contributed to that great book rightfully kept references to God broad. Nevertheless, they nearly continuously described Him as a "Higher Power."

Application:

Write about your relationship to the original AA literature. How do you feel about it? Do you own a copy of the *AA Big Book* yet? Do you have a *12&12*? If you don't, write about why you haven't gotten one yet. Do you feel a reluctance to owning these books? If so, why?

If you own an *AA Big Book*, take a special color of marking pen and begin to go through it, underlining the quotes that specifically encourage faith in God. Select one of these quotes and write about how it makes you feel.

4.4 2 Nephi 31:20—Wherefore, ye must press forward with a steadfastness in Christ, having a perfect brightness of *hope*...feasting upon the word of Christ (emphasis added).

A *perfect* brightness of hope is hope in the Lord Jesus Christ. Gaining hope His power and love in our lives is what "coming to believe" means. Having hope in Christ and *feasting* on the word of Christ gives us the ability to be steadfast instead of unstable.

Application:

In addition to pondering and praying, there are three ways to feast upon the word of Christ: read it, listen to it, and capture it.

Two of these ways, reading and listening, are forms of feasting on borrowed light—albeit of the highest quality. We receive this high-quality, high-powered borrowed light from the prophets through both their spoken and written messages to us. We should partake of such nourishment daily, realizing, however, that it is still borrowed.

Capturing is what makes such study our own revelation. (See What is Capturing? in the Appendix.) Write about capturing. Capturing is what you've been doing all through this study guide. In this likening process, you have felt wisdom greater than your own pour out along with your words.

Write your thoughts *about* capturing. How has it helped you to see into the meaning and depths of the scriptures? (And all else you read, too.)

4.5 Ether 12:12—For if there be no faith among the children of men God can do no miracle among them; wherefore, he showed not himself until after their faith.

Step Two is absolutely essential; it cannot be minimized or neglected. We can't transform ourselves, and neither can God without our belief. We are powerless without His power; and He is powerless, at least in our life, without our faith and agency. Without our faith in Him, God can do no miracle for us.

There are a variety of attitudes towards God and spirituality. One of the most heartbreaking is the addict "who means well and tries hard" but can't break loose from the bondage of their addictive problem (*12&12*, 32).

Many a bishop is sorely perplexed by the troubled members of their ward. Man or woman, sex addict, overeater, spendaholic or workaholic—they mean well and try hard. These people come back for interview after interview, set goal after goal, but nothing works. Yet their bishops have a sense that these are sincerely good people. Don't they have faith? What's the problem? Once again,

> The answer has to do with the quality of faith rather than its quantity (*12&12*, 32).

What is wrong with the quality of faith in a sincerely good member of the church, who is tying hard, who keeps coming back to church, to interviews, maybe even fills a calling or two?

The Book of Mormon teaches that exercising faith without the correct object, or target, for our faith will not call down the powers of God to help us resist evil:

> **Preach unto them repentance, and faith on the Lord Jesus Christ; teach them to humble themselves and to be meek and lowly in heart; teach them to withstand every temptation of the devil, with their faith on the Lord Jesus Christ (Alma 37:33).**

Faith in the Church, faith in the gospel, faith in our church leaders, faith in the scriptures, faith in ourselves—none of this faith goes far enough and deep enough to connect with the power of God. In fact, focusing on these things will keep us from our goal of recovery. The object of our faith *must* be the Lord Jesus Christ. Absolutely nothing short of this will do.

Application:

Ponder and prayerfully write your thoughts and reflections on the Savior's involvement in our exercise of faith. Only He can give us power sufficient to change our hearts, to redeem and recover us, to reconnect us with the glory from which we came.

Look in the Topical Guide under *Jesus Christ*. List some of the terms or names for Him. Look also in the Bible Dictionary under *Christ*. Write the meanings of *Emmanuel, Advocate,* and *Comforter* in your journal. Note the scriptures concerning this "other comforter," particularly **D&C 88:3–4**.

Write about the magnitude of His place in our salvation and the amazing grace of His Atonement.

4.6 Alma 15:6—Believest thou in the power of Christ unto salvation?

Now the question is: Are we ready to believe in His power? Our belief *releases* His power. And the wonderful truth is: Our belief doesn't have to be perfect.

Sometimes we need to see some results, some healing first, so our belief can grow stronger. This isn't a matter of seeking a sign, but rather is compatible with the teachings of Alma when he says that all we need to start with is a desire to believe **(Alma 32:27)**. This is the gospel equivalent of the Twelve Step slogan: "You just need to be willing to be willing." As Alma said, **"Let this desire work in you..."**.

Another scriptural example of the Lord's patience and longsuffering with our imperfect ability to believe is found when a man begged Him to heal his child. The Lord asked if he believed He could do this thing. The man replied, **"and said with tears, Lord, I believe; help thou mine unbelief" (Mark 9:24)**.

In humble honesty, this man admitted there was a portion of his attitude or belief system—and maybe the greater portion, for all we know—that didn't believe God could heal his child. And yet, the Lord was merciful toward him in his divided beliefs.

Recognition of our divided nature is also found in AA literature:

> Alcoholics Anonymous does not demand that you believe anything (*12&12*, 26).

This statement sounds so tolerant that, at first consideration, my all-or-nothing thinking could not accept it as a true principle. I was put off, almost offended. I have seen many a fellow Latter-day Saint leave Twelve Step programs over phrases like this. But there was a tolerance in this statement that was somehow Christ-like. Then, one day, I found why it felt so familiar to me.

In **Alma 32:27**, I found the same gentle spirit of persuasion, not of demanding: **"If ye can no more than desire to believe...".** Isn't this the same as not demanding a person believe anything to get started? And just like the seed growing into a tree in Alma's metaphor, the rest of the AA text unfolds:

> To get sober and to stay sober, you don't have to swallow all of Step Two right now... [but as they continued in the program] their faith broadened and...they came to believe in a Higher Power, and *most of them began to talk of God* (*12&12*, 26–28; emphasis added).

Application:

Ponder and write about this image of the Lord as patient, kind, and understanding of our human weaknesses. What effect does this view of Christ have upon you? Does it soften your heart? Are you becoming willing to believe that Christ is not only a Power greater than any other, but also a Power that is kinder and more loving than any you have ever known on earth?

4.7 Jacob 6:5—I beseech of you in words of soberness that ye would repent, and come with full purpose of heart, and cleave unto God as he cleaveth unto you.

These thoughts are echoed in AA literature:

> God will restore us to sanity *if we rightly relate ourselves to Him* (*12&12*, 33; emphasis added).

How do we "rightly relate ourselves" to God? Most people think of a proper relationship with God in terms of obedience. We tend to measure or evaluate a person's relationship with the Lord in terms of their outward, observable behavior. What we sometimes forget is that this outward behavior may not be a true manifestation of a person's love for, or connectedness with, the Lord.

The imagery of this scripture, of cleaving **"unto God as he cleaveth unto you,"** speaks of far more than a relationship based on obedience to authority. It speaks of love. A beautifully harmonious and enlightening cross-reference is **D&C 6:20**, which includes the heartening phrase, **"I will encircle thee in the arms of my love."**

In a First Presidency message, President James E. Faust affirmed the degree of intimacy symbolized in these scriptural words:

> We should earnestly seek not just to know about the Master, but to strive, as He invited, to be one with Him (see **John 17:21**), to "be strengthened with might by his Spirit in the inner man" **(Ephesians 3:16)** (*Ensign*, January 1999, 2).

Application:

Ponder and write about your previous picture of what a relationship with the Savior should be like. How did you perceive Him? Has this picture changed since beginning this course of study? If so, how?

Use your divine power of prayerful imaging and write about this theme: "If I could see the Savior again…" Include in your writing an acknowledgment of the truth that you knew Him in the premortal existence.

Supplemental Scriptures for Step Two

The following are additional scriptures which support Step Two:

1 Nephi 10:6—All mankind were in a lost and in a fallen state,...*save they should rely on this Redeemer* (emphasis added). Each of us must come to rely on Christ for our peace and serenity.

2 Nephi 6:14—The Messiah will...recover them;...when that day cometh when they shall believe in him; and none will he destroy that believe in him. Recovery and destruction of our enemies (our weaknesses and addictions) is the great promise that we are given when we shall come to "believe [in Him]."

2 Nephi 9:45—Come unto that God who is the rock of your salvation. Jesus Christ is the rock, or basis, of our salvation. All lesser gods—food, drugs, alcohol, sex, money, perfection, cleanliness, other people—are false gods which will eventually fail us.

2 Nephi 10:7—When the day cometh that they shall believe in me, that I am Christ, then have I covenanted with their fathers that they shall be restored in the flesh, *upon the earth* (emphasis added). This promise of restoration (recovery) is not only for some future celestial or millennial day. We can be restored to sanity here and now, in the flesh, upon the earth.

2 Nephi 20:12–15 In these verses the boastfulness and pride of the king of Assyria is rehearsed. He gives himself credit for his own success saying, **"By the strength of my hand and by my wisdom I have done these things; for I am prudent."** In reply, God asks, **"Shall the ax boast itself against him that heweth therewith?"** God is the one who moves "the borders" in our lives. We must acknowledge that He is in charge.

2 Nephi 25:28-29—I have spoken plainly unto you, that ye cannot misunderstand. ...the right way is to believe in Christ and deny him not;...ye must bow down before him, and worship him with all your might, mind, and strength, and your whole soul; and if ye do this ye shall in nowise be cast out. Nephi speaks to us very plainly about who our Higher Power is, how to believe in Him, and the lengths to which we must go for recovery.

2 Nephi 26:13—He manifesteth himself unto all those who believe in him, by the power of the Holy Ghost; yea, unto every nation, kindred, tongue, and people, working mighty miracles, signs, and wonders. We who need a miracle in our lives, need to know that Jesus Christ has all power and wisdom, and that in His strength we can do all things that are expedient for us.

Jarom 1:11—Believe in him...as though he already was. Just as belief comes *before* the miracle, faith in Christ *precedes* the miracle. Coming to believe precedes recovery.

Mosiah 4:6—If ye have come to a knowledge of the goodness of God, and his matchless power...that thereby salvation might come to him that should put his trust in the Lord. Salvation not only *might* come, it *will* come! We can trust in it. His power is matchless. There is no power to match it or thwart it. His purposes will be achieved.

Mosiah 4:8—And there is none other salvation. None. He will patiently wait while we try other paths to recovery, but sooner or later, all paths must lead to Him.

Mosiah 4:9—Believe in God; believe that he is, and that he created all things, both in heaven and in earth; believe that he has all wisdom, and all power, both in heaven and in earth; believe that man doth not comprehend all the things which the Lord can comprehend. God has all wisdom and all power. He knows how to break our cycle of addiction permanently and will share that knowledge with us.

Mosiah 5:7—Ye shall be called the children of Christ, his sons, and his daughters; for behold, this day he hath spiritually begotten you; for ye say that *your hearts are changed through faith on his name* (emphasis added). The mighty change is a change that is heart-deep. It is brought about by faith on the name of Jesus Christ.

Mosiah 11:23—Except this people repent and turn unto the Lord their God, they shall be brought into bondage; and none shall deliver them, except it be the Lord the Almighty God. We are in bondage when we are under the influence of any addiction or negative behavior, and only the Lord can and will deliver us.

Mosiah 24:21—For they were in bondage, and none could deliver them except it were the Lord their God. Note the words "the Lord their God." Only when the Lord becomes our God—our source of comfort and hope—can He deliver us from bondage.

Mosiah 25:16—They should remember that it was the Lord that did deliver them. When we forget that it is the Lord who delivers us, we fall back into bondage. We relapse. And just as soon as we acknowledge our loss of centeredness in Him and turn back with full purpose of heart, He will respond and put us back on the path of recovery.

Mosiah 27:25-26—All mankind, yea, men and women... must be born again; yea, born of God...being redeemed of God....And thus they become new creatures. Alma's testimony from the Lord is that all of us need this rebirth experience. It is this redemption of Jesus Christ which makes us new creatures and restores us to sanity.

Alma 13:28—Humble yourselves before the Lord. The words "greater than ourselves" in Step Two are keys to this humility. To continue to struggle alone with our addiction is the equivalent of saying we choose to put our hope of salvation in ourselves.

Alma 19:36—His arm is extended to all people who will repent and believe on his name. All people, even us.

Alma 22:16—If thou desirest this thing, if thou wilt bow down before God, yea, if thou wilt repent of all thy sins, and will bow down before God, and call on his name in faith, believing that ye shall receive, then shalt thou receive the hope which thou desirest. The promise to Aaron is a promise to us as well. If we work these steps, we will receive that hope which we desire.

Alma 26:12—I will boast of my God, for in his strength I can do all things. This is the other half of Ammon's statement about his nothingness (see Step 1). It is also the other half of the equation for us.

Alma 32:22—God is merciful unto all who believe on his name; therefore he desireth, in the first place, that ye should believe, yea, even on his word. Coming to believe in His word, through ancient and modern prophets, and as revealed directly to our own hearts and minds, is one way we can believe on His name and tap into His power.

Alma 32:27—If ye will awake and arouse your faculties, even to an experiment upon my words, and exercise a particle of faith, yea, even if ye can no more than desire to believe, let this desire work in you. If we can't come to believe completely, we can be willing to be willing. Even a particle of faith will grow.

Alma 34:15—And thus he shall bring salvation to all those who shall believe on his name; this being the intent of this last sacrifice, to bring about the bowels of mercy, which overpowereth justice, and bringeth about means unto men that they may have faith unto repentance. Those of us who have feared a judgmental, angry God need fear no more. Christ has atoned, allowing mercy to overpower justice for those who repent and turn to Him.

Alma 37:33—Withstand every temptation...with their faith on the Lord Jesus Christ. We will only be able to withstand every temptation if our faith and hope of recovery is in Christ.

Alma 37:47—Look to God and live...be sober. Simply looking to God will bring me the life and sobriety I desire.

Alma 38:9—There is no other way or means whereby man can be saved, only in and through Christ. Once again, Alma makes the solution to the problem of gaining salvation from addiction, as well as from any other affliction, perfectly clear.

Alma 42:27—Whosoever will come may come and partake of the waters of life freely; and whosoever will not come the same is not compelled to come. Restoration to sanity is a gift offered freely to all, contingent only upon our willingness to accept the gift.

Alma 55:31—The Nephites were not slow to remember the Lord their God in this their time of affliction. They could not be taken in their snares. Protection and peace come from remembering the Lord, even in times of affliction. Taking Step Two is the equivalent of being willing to remember God and turn to Him in our need.

Alma 58:11—The Lord our God did visit us with assurances that he would deliver us; yea, insomuch that he did speak peace to our souls, and did grant unto us great faith, and did cause us that we should hope for our deliverance in him. Faith in Jesus Christ is a gift. If we lack this gift, we can pray to receive it. If we're struggling to "come to believe," we can ask the Lord to help us with our faith.

Alma 58:33, 37—We trust in our God who has given us victory...we trust God will deliver us. As we watch the power of God do for us what we can't do for ourselves, in regard to the original problem that brought us to a Twelve Step program, we can begin to trust that He can give us victory in other areas of life as well.

Helaman 3:27-28—Thus we may see that the Lord is merciful unto all who will, in the sincerity of their hearts, call upon his holy name...the gate of heaven is open unto all, even to those who will believe on the name of Jesus Christ, who is the Son of God. The gate of heaven—recovery and sanity—is open to all who believe.

Helaman 4:13—And because of...their boastings in their own strength, they were left in their own strength; therefore they did not prosper. Our own strength is never enough. It cannot cause us to prosper.

Helaman 5:12—It is upon the rock of our Redeemer, who is Christ, the Son of God, that ye must build your foundation. Our recovery can include individual therapy, support groups, medical intervention, and many other pathways, but all must be built on the foundation of Christ. To withstand any addiction or depression, the rock of our Redeemer is our sure foundation.

Helaman 5:47—Peace be unto you, because of your faith in my Well Beloved. Peace, or sanity, is a result of believing in Christ as a Power greater than yourself.

Helaman 7:17—Turn ye, turn ye unto the Lord your God. In other words, take Step Two.

Helaman 12:24—And may God grant, in his great fulness, that men might be brought unto repentance and good works, that they might be restored unto grace for grace, according to their works. The gift we must ask for, just as Mormon does, is that we might be restored, or recovered, by the grace of God. Also that we might be able to perform good works, which ability is also a gift.

3 Nephi 4:10—Yea, in the strength of the Lord they did receive [their enemies]. When we receive attacks from our worst enemies—our temptations and weaknesses— we must receive them in the strength of our Higher Power, Jesus Christ, or we will not prevail.

Ether 3:4—And I know, O Lord, that thou hast all power, and can do whatsoever thou wilt for the benefit of man; therefore touch these stones, O Lord…that they may shine forth in darkness. How like common stones the lives of addicts are, as they stumble along, their hearts hardened by sin. But how different those same lives become when the miracle of belief in God's infinite power, and hope in His infinite goodness, ignites in their hearts.

Ether 12:41—I would commend you to seek this Jesus of whom the prophets and apostles have written, that the grace of God the Father, and also the Lord Jesus Christ, and the Holy Ghost, which beareth record of them, may be and abide in you forever. Step Two, "coming to believe," is in its very essence the act of seeking "this Jesus" who will redeem us from our addictions.

Moroni 7:3—Ye can enter into the rest of the Lord, from this time henceforth. To "enter into the rest of the Lord" describes being restored to sanity in the highest degree possible to mortal man.

Moroni 7:42—Wherefore, if a man have faith he must needs have hope; for without faith there cannot be any hope. Unless we come to believe in a power greater than ourselves, there is no hope that we can be restored to sanity.

Moroni 8:3—That he, through his infinite goodness and grace, will keep you through the endurance of faith on his name to the end. Here is yet another statement of the eternal equation for a recovery which will endure to the end: His infinite goodness and grace, unleashed by our faith on Him and His name.

Moroni 10:32—Yea, come unto Christ...then is his grace sufficient for you. His grace is sufficient for each of us.

Other References for Step Two

As you find other references to Step Two in your personal daily scripture study, list them here:

Step Three

Made the decision to turn our will and our lives over to the care of God as we understood Him. Made the decision to reconcile ourselves to the will of God, offer our whole souls as an offering unto Him, and trust Him in all things, forever.

As we contemplate Step Three, most of us will experience one or the other of two reactions. Some of us recoil in terror, clutching our divine agency to ourselves. Others of us stall out in sheer bewilderment, staggered by the magnitude of the task. "Never!" cry some; others ask, "But how?"

> Practicing Step Three is like the opening of a door which to all appearances is still closed and locked (12&12, 34).

Practicing. We might as well start this in-depth study of Step Three by considering the accuracy of the very first word in AA's official discussion of this step. That one word—*practicing*—is the key to understanding how to take Step Three.

Practicing doesn't mean doing it 100% of the time. Practicing doesn't mean perfection. Practicing, according to the *Oxford American Dictionary*, means "to do something repeatedly in order to become skillful."

Recovery begins when we are willing to practice it.

We have to be willing to be crummy at something before we can get better at it.

Closed and locked. It might be good for us to stop and ponder this phrase by asking ourselves, "If Step Three is like a closed and locked door, what is it that is keeping it closed and locked to *me*?" Is it my fear, my pride, my self-will or self-pity?

The door of Step Three swings open quite freely, actually, but it opens inward, *toward me*. If something is keeping it closed, it is on my side of the door, not God's.

I will never forget the first time the Lord showed this truth to me. It was as if I could hear Him saying, *"Colleen, the truth is there are no locks on the prison door of your addiction."*

There didn't need to be any outer locks to keep the door shut because I was, myself, preventing the inward swing of the door with blocks of denial, resistance, shame and blame. He showed me that I must let go of life and surrender to its reality, that I must retreat a little and relax to give room for the door to open in my life.

I must be willing to take Step Three by surrendering to the truth that I am in bondage, whether by my own hand or the hand of others who introduced me to sin. I must release my death grip of resistance and regret, of resentment and rage, from the iron bars of my current imprisoned state. I must step back in patience and humility, in acceptance and contriteness of heart.

When I stop pushing and shoving, lying and denying life on life's terms (which, whether I like it or not, includes the results of both my own mistakes and the mistakes others have committed against me), the door blocking my progress in Step Three opens "almost of itself" (*12&12*, 34).

> There is only one key, and it is called willingness (*12&12*, 34).

Where have we Latter-day Saints heard this concept before? If it sounds familiar to us, there's a good reason.

> **Yea, even if ye can no more than desire to believe, let this desire work in you, even until ye believe (Alma 32:27).**

In this verse, Alma tells us that a *desire* to believe is sufficient to start the process. And so it is with this fearful, seemingly overwhelming task of opening the door of our lives to the will of the Lord. God waits upon our desire, our willingness. God waits upon our decision. He must.

In **Doctrine and Covenants 121:41**, we are told that no power or influence *can* be maintained by virtue of the priesthood, but only by such influences as patience, long-suffering, *persuasion* and love unfeigned. God models this behavior in His own interaction with us, His children.

The verses from the Book of Mormon that we will study for Step Three, are just about the purest form of persuasion God can offer us. He stands and waits for us to make the decision to surrender our will and our lives to Him. All He needs is our decision, our permission and He will begin to take the slums out of us, as President Benson once put it:

> The Lord works from the inside out. The world works from the outside in. The world would take people out of the slums. Christ takes the slums out of people, and then they take themselves out of the slums. The world would mold men by changing their

> environment. Christ changes men, who then change their environment. The world would shape human behavior, but Christ can change human nature (Ezra T. Benson, *Teachings of Ezra Taft Benson*, 1988, 79).

He stands at the door and knocks, but only we can let Him in.

Step Three—Week One

1.1 Alma 26:12—I know that I am nothing…I will boast of my God, for in his strength I can do all things.

This is the scriptural version of the famous summary of the first three steps: "I can't. God can. I'll let Him." As noted in Step One, many people balk at this need to admit powerlessness or nothingness. They criticize Twelve Step recovery, crying, "What can you possibly be thinking? How can you tell us we're *powerless*, when we so desperately need to be *empowered*?"

What these people do not recognize is the familiar pattern of paradox so plainly taught by the Savior Himself when He stated that a person must lose their life *for His sake* to find it **(Matthew 10:39)**. The whole purpose of Steps One and Two is to clear away enough of our own ego to make room for a *really* effective Source of Power to find place in us.

Read Ammon's words again. Does it sound like Ammon feels powerless because of his knowledge that he is nothing? No. The exact opposite. Ammon has come to realize that there are many problems and challenges in life that "will not yield to a headlong assault powered by the individual alone" (*12&12*, 40).

This truth is empowering. Ammon knows when to stop an unproductive cycle, when to give up on getting nowhere and turn to God for His power. **"For in *HIS* strength I can do all things."** You can't get more empowered than that!

Application:

Ponder and write about how the first three steps are individual principles and, at the same time, all part of one mighty flow of truth. Write out the slogan, "I can't. God can. I'll let Him." Focus on the meaning of letting God empower you His way.

What challenges—weaknesses, trials, setbacks, sorrows, disappointments—have you tried to overcome with a headlong assault? What was the result?

1.2 2 Nephi 10:24—Reconcile yourselves to the will of God.

Often we think of the word "reconcile" in a negative way, picturing someone who is reconciled as just going along with something in a grudging spirit. The dictionary, however, gives the following definitions for reconcile:

> To restore to friendship or harmony. To make consistent or congruous.

To reconcile ourselves to the will of God does not mean we must bow before the lash of hated and despised circumstances. It is to open our hearts and pray, in our own heart and in our own words, in the same spirit as the "Third Step prayer":

> God, I offer myself to Thee...Relieve me of the bondage of self, that I may better do Thy will (*AA*, 63).

When we pray with this kind of surrender, we open our minds to God's will. He can then reveal to us His benevolent intent in allowing us our challenges and the potential growth we can experience from them.

Under God's guidance, we can truly see our circumstances as He sees them and allow our will to become His. Only then are we truly reconciled.

Application:

For most of us, it is a great leap of faith to make the decision to let go of our own will. It is a challenge to believe and trust that the way things work out is a manifestation of God's benevolence. Ponder and write about this decision in your life.

Think of something in your life that you're reluctant to be reconciled with, something you're learning you have no power to change. Write honestly about your reality. Can you believe there is a benevolent purpose in your challenge? If so, what is this purpose? If not, write about your level of willingness to have a benevolent purpose revealed to you.

1.3 Omni 1:26—Offer your whole souls as an offering unto him.

How much plainer can it be stated? Our *whole* soul—body and spirit. This is the ultimate act of consecration. It is to come full circle back to God and offer to Him all that He's given us. Not just a tithe or a portion, but *everything*. It is to consecrate unto Him the one thing that He did not create—our sovereign agency or will. My will is my gift to God. His power is His gift to me.

Still, it can be terrifying to make such a complete surrender. Some of us may have feelings similar to this alcoholic:

> Nothing is going to turn me into a nonentity. If I keep on turning my life and my will over to the care of Something or Somebody else, what will become of me? I'll look like the hole in the doughnut (*12&12*, 36; emphasis original).

We often feel fear and resistance at **"offering our whole souls as an offering"** to God.

Application:

Ponder and write about the fact that you are an eternal entity endowed by God with a spirit body and, more recently, a physical body **(D&C 93:29)**. How does it make you feel to know there is something only you can give to the Lord—your willingness (will)?

There may be men or women who have exercised unrighteous dominion over your soul. Can you believe that the Lord Jesus Christ and our Heavenly Father are not among them? Can you believe that they do not approve of such dominion, though They allow it for eternally important purposes? Write a letter to Heavenly Father expressing your thoughts, fears or feelings concerning this concept.

1.4 1 Nephi 8:5-10—I saw a man...dressed in a white robe...and [he] bade me follow him.

Lehi says he saw a man dressed in a white robe who bade him to follow Him. He trusted the man and followed him. Eventually, Lehi was led to the tree of life, but where did he go first?

Application:

Picture yourself in Lehi's place. A man dressed in white comes and stands before you and bids you to follow Him. Who do you think the man is? Do you follow Him? Why? Do you think He warned us that to follow Him would involve risk and the trials?

What act of faith must we, like Lehi, take in order to see our circumstances in a different light (see v. 8)?

1.5 Mosiah 3:19—Willing to submit to all things which the Lord seeth fit to inflict upon him.

Often we rage against an injustice, justifying our choice to be enraged by declaring, "This is not right! It's not fair! God would never allow this to happen!"

Yet the scriptures are replete with testimony that God has all power in heaven and earth and holds all within His hand. From the very first scene in the garden, God has allowed evil to exist on this earth. Sometimes He has inspired people to attack the evil head-on and eliminate it. Other times he has allowed evil to continue unimpeded **(Alma 14:11)**.

Application:

Ponder and prayerfully write about what the world would be like if God used His power to immediately eliminate all evil.

Read **Alma 14:11** again and write down the two reasons why God allows injustice to happen. What does He promise the victims? What does it say about the perpetrators?

1.6 Mormon 7:4—Lay down your weapons of war…and take them not again, save it be that God shall command you.

Like those early alcoholics who "have ceased fighting anything or anyone" (*AA*, 85), we must be willing to allow God to prescribe for us when, where, and how we conduct our lives, even in the defense of our physical lives **(Alma 24:16)**.

We must put our time and energy into loving God and trying to follow His counsel in all things forever.

Application:

It is a natural, knee-jerk reaction to defend ourselves when we've been wronged. Defending ourselves is not always wrong. The secret is to do it *when the Lord commands us* to do it and only then.

Prayerfully write about the challenge to look to the Lord, even in angry moments, and to seek His counsel as to whether to stand up for ourselves or to let the situation go. Write about your feelings concerning the statement:

> If we were to live, we had to be free of anger. The grouch and the brainstorm [as in fits of anger]... these things are poison (*AA*, 66).

1.7 Helaman 10:4—Thou hast not feared them, and hast not sought thine own life, but hast sought my will.

In the Joseph Smith Translation of **Matthew 10:39,** the Savior makes this statement:

> **He who seeketh to save his life shall lose it; and he that loseth his life for my sake shall find it.**

Here, in Helaman, we find further understanding of just how it is that a person can lose his life for Christ. To turn our will over to God and to seek to do His will instead is most definitely a way of losing our life for His sake.

Application:

Ponder and prayerfully write about giving up your ideas of how life should be, how it should turn out. How does sincerely saying, "Dear God, Thy will be done," help you live the *meaning* of the Savior's words.

Write about a circumstance or situation in your life where you had to give up your life by giving up your will, where you had to "abandon [yourself] utterly to Him" (*AA*, 63).

Step Three—Week Two

2.1 Alma 37:36—Cry unto God for all thy support...*all* thy doings...*all* thy thoughts (emphasis added).

I do not hear these words say, Cry unto the Lord for *most* of my support, and then get the rest from spouse, or family, or friends, or food, or looking good, etc. I do not hear these words say that only *some portion* of my doings or only *some percentage* of my thoughts should be done prayerfully. I hear these words say *all* my doings and *all* my thoughts are to be done in a spirit of crying unto the Lord, of coming before the Lord.

> **Let the affections of thy heart be placed upon the Lord *forever* (Alma 37:36; emphasis added).**

The affections of my heart are my deepest, most central and vital affections. They are to be placed on the Lord—every minute, day and night. Not just in the morning, for a bit of private time with Him and His Word, but all day long, as I do everything else.

Application:

Ponder and prayerfully write about this word, *affection*. Where have the affections of *your* heart been placed over the years?

In Twelve Step programs, we are warned against "all or nothing" thinking and attitudes. The one place where "all" is appropriate is in giving all your heart and life to God. Write about the ways in your life in which you are successfully giving your all to God. Write about ways that you could improve.

2.2 1 Nephi 20:2—[We must] stay [ourselves] upon the God of Israel.

This is an old fashioned use of the word "stay." It means "to remain, to continue, to endure." Sometimes it takes a great deal of trust to stay with a friend when the going gets tough, particularly in situations when there may be evidence or witnesses condemning them. But this word, *stay*, embodies how we must remain with God—trusting Him, even when all evidence seems to condemn Him for being unkind or uncaring. Trusting God *in all things* is the highest form of worship and affection we can show Him.

Application:

Think of a time where you were tempted to interpret a situation or experience in your life as proof that God didn't love you. What are your feelings now, as you look back at those circumstances? Write a narrative of that experience from your current perspective.

2.3 Alma 5:13—They humbled themselves and put their trust in the true and living God.

Humility is a choice **(Alma 32:16)**. We often think that the afflictions we suffer humble us, but this is not entirely accurate. We either choose to humble ourselves in reaction to the things that happen to us, or we don't.

> I am the result of the *way I reacted* to what happened to me as a child (*AA*, 544; emphasis original).

Application:

Ponder and write about the idea that humility is a choice. What are some of the other reactions we can choose to have concerning a difficult life experience?

These hard moments are our proving ground. Even if we have been rebellious in the past, we can begin today to choose a new way to react. Finish the sentence: "Today, I choose to react to ___________ [insert a specific person or experience] by ___________." Prayerfully select and describe a reaction that is different from one you have chosen in the past.

Continue to write about how you might choose to react differently today. Who do you think is willing to help you make different choices?

2.4 Mosiah 24:15—They did submit cheerfully and with patience to all the will of the Lord.

> The only real freedom a human being can ever know is doing what you ought to do because you want to do it (*AA*, 552).

To do the right thing with the wrong attitude "profiteth [us] nothing" (Moroni 7:6-9). Our ultimate result in practicing this principle is to learn to trust God enough to sing His praises even while we are in circumstances that feel like a prison. (See the story of Paul and Silas, **Acts 16:16–34**; specifically verse 25.)

Application:

Notice the word "practicing." Practicing is not perfection. In fact, in the beginning, practicing is what you call virtually zero experience and total ignorance. If that's where you feel like you are with this step, if trusting God with your life scares you, say so. Write about it. Write the Lord a letter expressing how many layers of "willing to be willing" still separate you from being able to submit cheerfully to the sorrowful things in your life.

2.5 Mormon 9:20—He ceaseth to do miracles...because [they] ...know not the God in whom they should trust.

According to this scripture, there is a relationship between the number of miracles we experience and how well we know and trust God. If we do not believe in Divine help, we will not be looking for it. We will see positive events or circumstances as coincidences. In such a mind-set of doubt and disbelief, we aren't very likely to listen to, or experiment upon, His promise to carry us through to a miraculous solution when we are confronted with a problem **(Alma 32:27)**.

Application:

Make a list of changes—in people, places, circumstances—that would feel like miracles if they were to happen. Select one or two items on your list and write about them in some detail. Express to God why you would like to have a certain outcome. Tell Him your will and then give your will to Him.

(If you want to learn from the unfolding story of your life's opportunities, check back on these same issues in a few months. Write about the changes that have taken place.)

2.6 1 Nephi 7:12—Yea, and how is it that ye have forgotten that the Lord is able to do all things according to his will, for the children of men, if it so be that they exercise faith in him? Wherefore, let us be faithful to him.

I've believed that God could do whatever He wanted, when He wanted, in a sort of arbitrary and obviously omnipotent way. I didn't realize that He had boundaries and circumstances to which He must surrender His will and power. Deeper study of the scriptures of the Restoration seems to indicate that there is one influence that limits God's ability or power: *our faith, or lack of it*.

Those who choose to resist exercising faith in God do not receive the fullness of God's blessings. This is not because God withholds His blessings and power from us as a punishment, but because the pathway for delivery of these blessings is blocked by our lack of faith in Him.

> Practicing Step Three is like the opening of a door which to all appearances is still closed and locked. All we need is a key, and the decision to swing the door open. There is only one key…willingness. … "This is the way to a faith that works" (*12&12,* 34).

We *need* a faith that will connect us with the Power to take action on our desire to stop practicing our addiction.

Application:

Prayerfully write your thoughts concerning this adjustment in understanding the omnipotence of God. For other scriptural references, you may want read and capture from **Ezekiel 35:11; Mosiah 26:26; Alma 26:35; Helaman 3:29; D&C 1:11; D&C 21:6; D&C 88:32**. How does this new understanding impact your affection for God? Does it help to realize that His desire to bless His children is constant, but that He cannot cross their choice or agency?

2.7 2 Nephi 25:23—For we know that it is by grace that we are saved, after all we can do.

There was a time in my life when the words "after all [you] can do" threw me into a pit of despair. How could I tell when I had really done *all* I could do? *Surely,* I thought, *I can do more—at least until unconsciousness overtakes me.*

I drove myself to continue, doing more and more, using my addiction like a wild person to keep myself going. But no matter what I did, it never seemed to be enough. I was overwhelmed. I felt like such a failure. I was angry with and mean-spirited to everyone around me.

Then one day while reading and capturing, I found the answer in **D&C 123:17**. In the midst of that verse, I found the key to knowing when I had reached my limit of "all I can do" and could rightfully call on Divine intervention: When I can no longer go on *cheerfully.*

Today, when I feel that my ability to be of good cheer has been pushed to its limit, I call a halt—just like the slogan in Twelve Step recovery recommends. I inventory my truth. Have I let myself get too hungry, angry, lonely, or tired?

If I have, then I need to admit my limitations. I must stand still, and let God carry the ball until I get the rest I need to tackle the challenge again.

The principle taught in **D&C 123:17** is echoed in the Serenity Prayer:

> In all times of emotional disturbance or indecision [or exhaustion], we can pause, ask for quiet, and in the stillness simply say: "God grant me the serenity to accept the things I cannot change, courage to change the things I can, and wisdom to know the difference. Thy will, not mine, by done" (*12&12*, 41).

Application:

Prayerfully ponder and write about how you feel about this idea of doing all you can do before you can expect the grace (power) of God to come to your aid.

Open your scriptures to **D&C 123:17** and read it side by side with the Serenity Prayer. Write about the harmony you see in the ideas they contain.

Step Three—Week Three

3.1 Helaman 3:35—Nevertheless they did fast and pray oft, and did wax stronger and stronger in their humility, and firmer and firmer in the faith of Christ,

unto the filling their souls with joy and consolation, yea, even to the purifying and the sanctification of their hearts, which sanctification cometh because of their yielding their hearts unto God.

This verse is a perfect synthesis of some of the most powerful principles and practices in the Twelve Step program: humility, prayer, faith (trust) in Christ (God, as we understand Him), and the turning of our will over to Him.

Application:

Prayerfully ponder and write about the process outlined in this verse. Identify the actions they took and the results they obtained from these actions.

Ponder and write about the similarity between abstaining from an addiction and fasting, an act that removes our dependency from things of this world and puts us in touch with the "true independence of the spirit" that comes from dependency on God (*12&12*, 36).

3.2 **Jacob 4:7—The Lord God showeth us our weakness that we may know that it is by his grace, and his great condescensions…that we have** [any] **power…**

There is a thought common to virtually every addict, regardless of the focus of their addiction:

> Yes, respecting [this weakness, my addictive problem] I guess I have to be dependent on [God, help from others], but in all other

> matters I must still maintain my independence (*12&12*, 36).

What we do not realize is that *everything* in our life that looks okay is also being given to us by God. What we don't realize is that our *whole lives* would be in as much chaos as our addictive problems, if it weren't for God's help and empowerment.

Those areas we consider to be our weaknesses are, in actuality, our windows into what all of existence would be like without the condescension of God.

Application:

Look up the word "condescend" in the dictionary. What does it mean? How has God made a great condescension in your behalf? What do you think motivates Him? Write about His patient nature and His willingness to wait for you to understand this concept.

3.3 Alma 29:9—I know that which the Lord hath commanded me, and I glory in it.

> Acceptance is the answer to *all* my problems...I can find no serenity until I accept that [everything is] exactly the way it is supposed to be at this moment.... Unless I accept life completely on life's terms, I cannot be happy (*AA*, 449; emphasis original).

That is powerful counsel, although I've often thought it should read "accepting life on *Life's* terms" (note the capital 'L').

A synonymous thought comes earlier in this chapter:

> **For I ought to be content with the things which the Lord hath allotted unto me (Alma 29:3).**

To glory in what the Lord has commanded me, to be content with that which the Lord has allotted to me, and to accept life on Life's (His) terms, are all compatible statements. They are also harmonious with that portion of the Serenity Prayer which says, "God grant me the serenity to accept the things I cannot change."

Serenity comes from acceptance of what Life commands us. We must learn to go gently through life. If it cannot be changed by those means listed in **D&C 121:41–42**, then it is something that is not within our righteous power to change.

Application:

Make a list of circumstances in which you have been commanded by life. In other words, list the things you've had to face, things you could not change or avoid.

The death of my oldest daughter was one of those. That event was not a suggestion from life, or an optional requirement. It was the equivalent of a definite, irrevocable command.

Select one of these experiences and write a short essay about it, as if you were telling me your story.

3.4 Alma 26:35—My joy is carried away, even unto boasting in my God; for he has all power, all wisdom, and all understanding; he comprehendeth all things, *and he is a merciful Being* (emphasis added).

In this statement, boasting is a synonym for exulting, glorying, praising, rejoicing in my God. (Notice the personal possessive pronoun: *my*.)

Ammon, like Nephi in **2 Nephi 33:6**, refers to God with tender intimacy. Ammon has come to know God and he rejoices in that knowledge. He boasts to others that: (1) God has all power, and in His power, after we accept His will over ours, we can do all things that are expedient; and (2) God has all wisdom, all understanding, and He comprehends all things. All the more reason for us to surrender our will and lives to Him.

Finally, and most important of all, Ammon has learned that the God of his understanding is a merciful Being.

Reference to this God is also found in the *AA Big Book*:

> Even so has God restored us all to our right minds. To [some], the revelation [that

> brings a mighty change] was sudden. Some of us grow into it more slowly. But He has come to all who have honestly sought Him. When we drew near to Him He disclosed Himself to us! (*AA*, 57).

Application:

Oh, how important it is to understand that the God of the Book of Mormon—the God of the Restoration of the Gospel of Jesus Christ—is a merciful God. Ponder and prayerfully write about your past conception of God. Was He merciful? Or was He strict and punishing? Write about your willingness to allow the image of a strict and punishing God to be replaced by a merciful one.

3.5 3 Nephi 10:6—How oft will I gather you…if ye will repent and return unto me.

In this verse, as in **Mosiah 26:30**, we receive testimony of Christ's mercy towards us. Christ lives by the same standard He requires of priesthood leaders, outlined in **D&C 121:41-43**. In light of these verses, we begin to understand the meaning of these words:

> **And if any man hear my words, and believe not, I judge him not: for I came not to judge the world, but to save the world (John 12:47).**

Someday, the Lord will have to (reluctantly and with great sorrow, I believe) sit in judgment over the world—but right now, I testify to you, *He has not come to judge you, but to save you.*

Application:

One of the hardest things to turn over to God is our desire to be perfect. For years, while I practiced my addiction, I desperately wanted to stop—and I wanted to stop perfectly, immediately, instantly. That same defect that wanted *instant* relief from my pain—the defect that created my compulsive, addictive behavior—also wanted *instant* recovery.

Can you relate to this way of thinking? Write about your willingness to start where you are and to be as merciful towards yourself as the Savior is. If you are honestly trying, He's willing to forgive you over and over. Write about your willingness to accept imperfection in yourself and to keep coming back.

3.6 Mosiah 7:33—But if ye will turn to the Lord with full purpose of heart, and put your trust in him, and serve him with all diligence of mind, if ye do this, he will, according to his own will and pleasure, deliver you out of bondage.

We are required to wait upon the Lord—even in this business of getting our life in order. We must accept that we will get fixed, cleaned up, sobered up, and totally delivered according to His own will and pleasure. That means, *not* when it would suit us or make us happy.

You might ask, "But why?" What purpose would He have for not wanting to perfect me, immediately, the moment I am finally, *truly* willing to come to Him? Even in timing, we must learn to wait upon the Lord.

> We had to quit playing God. It didn't work… In this drama of life, God was going to be *our* Director…this concept was the keystone of the new and triumphant arch through which we [could pass] to freedom (*AA*, 62, emphasis added).

Application:

Ponder this idea of our weaknesses being removed gradually. Sometimes, if our addiction is one that is especially damaging to ourself or others, we can't afford to take a gradual approach to stopping. We have to stop immediately.

Prayerfully ponder and write about your addiction and whether it is one that could rob, or has robbed, you of your Church membership or temple worthiness. Or is your challenge one that allows you some leeway for gradual change?

Sometimes, when people are recovering from more destructive addictions, they will slide into a "lesser" addiction. This lesser problem allows them to continue the process of learning more about their addictive nature and how to surrender it completely to the Savior. Have you had that experience? Write about it.

3.7 2 Nephi 31:19—Relying wholly upon the merits of him who is mighty to save.

Christ is the **"Holy *One* of Israel" (2 Nephi 30:2; Omni 1:26**; emphasis added). There is only one Person who ever lived on this earth who was able to keep it together, able to remain *whole* (and thus holy) while under the influence of the evil in this world. Only Christ.

There is not one other single soul who has been able to remain pure and holy through a lifetime upon this earth. Everyone else who has come to this earth has fallen short of this degree of glory **(Romans 3:23)**.

Since this is true, what hope do I have, mortal as I am and surrounded by nothing but other mortals in this world? I must look beyond the help of this mortal, tangible world to the invisible but very real Power of the Spirit of God.

> Silently and surely, electricity, that strange energy so few people understand [but which we all trust continually], meets our simplest daily needs, and our most desperate ones, too (*12&12*, 36).

Why do I find it so hard to trust in the invisible power of Him who is **"mighty to save"**? Only in Him is there certainty and assurance.

This program of recovery invites me to *practice* dependency upon the Lord. It encourages me to learn to rely *wholly* upon the only One who deserves that kind of loyalty, the only One who merits that kind of dependence from me.

Application:

Ponder and prayerfully write about your history of dependence. Who and what have you been dependent upon over the course of your life? How do you feel about being wholly dependent on Christ, even if He chooses to remain invisible to you? Are you ready to shift all your loyalty to Him? Yes? No? Why or why not?

Step Three—Week Four

4.1 1 Nephi 18:11—The Lord did suffer it that he might show forth his power.

Here is another instance of the idea we considered in Step Two. The Lord suffers (or allows) negative things to happen in mortality for His long-range, eternal purposes.

Three other instances of this truth are found in **Genesis 45:8** (Joseph assures his brothers it was not they, but rather *God*, who sent him into Egypt), **John 9:3** (the Savior corrects those who think that affliction is a punishment for sin), and **Alma 14:11** (the Spirit constrains Alma and Amulek from rescuing the innocent women and children).

How do we trust a God who *allows* these things happen? Read **2 Nephi 2:11–13** for a clue as to why God allows this to happen.

Application:

Read the verses cited in today's study. Prayerfully ponder and write, seeking the truth concerning these things. Write about the idea that God—though He is omnipotent—must use that power according to principles by which even He must abide.

Are you willing to consider that: (1) all things are working together for our good; and (2) the way things happen in life are not determined by God's love or lack of love for us, but by our choices and His eternal purposes? How does it make you feel to think that He has the wisdom and the foresight to weave even our worst choices into His eternal purposes?

4.2 Jacob 4:10—Seek not to counsel the Lord.

When we finally surrender our lives and our will to God, we begin to pray in a whole new way. Our prayers begin to have less emphasis on what we *want*, and more emphasis on what would be *best*—whatever that may be. We begin to trust the outcome to God. We find ourselves not counseling the Lord by asking for specific things, but counseling with Him about what He would have us have, do and be.

One of the most beautiful testimonies of seeking to do God's will in all things comes from Bill Wilson, co-founder of AA:

> I was to test my thinking by the new God-consciousness within. Common sense would thus become uncommon sense. I was to sit quietly when in doubt, asking only for direction and strength to meet my problems as He would have me…
>
> My friend promised when these things were done I would enter upon a new relationship with my Creator; that I would have the elements of a way of living which answered all my problems. Belief in the power of God, plus enough willingness, honesty and humility to establish and maintain the new order of things, were the essential requirements.
>
> Simple, but not easy; a price had to be paid. It meant destruction of self-centeredness. I must turn in all things to the Father of Light who presides over us all (*AA*, 13-14).

It takes some of us a long time to realize that Alma 37:37 doesn't say *"Counsel the Lord in all thy doings,"* but says instead, "Counsel *with* the Lord."

Application:

Ponder and write about this mighty change of focus in prayer. What does it feel like to try on the idea of "praying only for a knowledge of His will for [you, not your child or spouse or other] and the power to carry that out" (Step 11)?

Can you see the way that this program helps us to prepare to be "at-one" with the Lord? Write about what it means in your life to be "at-one" (as one) with the Savior's heart and mind. What does this imply about your relationship with the Father, since He and the Savior are as one in all things?

4.3 Moroni 10:23—If ye have faith ye can do all things which are expedient unto me.

With those words, **"which are expedient unto me,"** God retains the right to the driver's seat, the director's chair, and most especially, as we mentioned earlier, the time clock. The word "expedient" means "what is opportune in a given circumstance, what is useful at a certain time."

Often we become impatient, wanting to see all trials and challenges taken away *right now*. We desperately need to accept His timing and to trust that there is a purpose in it. There is safety in doing so.

The truth is, we could be downright dangerous if He gave us His power to move mountains, raise the dead or even lift our own or others' burdens if we are not humble enough to trust His timing. How grateful we should be that somewhere, long ago, we all consented to let Him be in charge.

Application:

Ponder and prayerfully record your thoughts concerning this idea that we consented to let the Lord be in charge. Write about the security it does (or could) give you to know that someone whose memory isn't veiled (like our minds are) is guiding and orchestrating all our lives, all at once, so the timing is perfect and for the good of all.

4.4 2 Nephi 31:20 —Press forward with a steadfastness in Christ.

"Keep coming back! It works!" This slogan is repeated at the end of many Twelve Step meetings. I used to think "it" referred to some elusive something, which, if I kept coming back, I might find and thus be suddenly cured of my addiction. Then came the day when I realized the "it" that works is the principle of "coming back."

In other words, "Keep coming back! Coming back works!" This same principle is expressed in the words, **"Press forward with a steadfastness in Christ."** I once heard someone say, "Don't give up when you fall on your face. At least you're moving forward." It is the continued forward motion, the steadfastness, that works.

The hope we have in being steadfast and not giving up must be centered in Jesus Christ and His power to redeem us, not hope in our own wavering human performance. We can't quit just because we struggle. Of course we're going to struggle! Yes, we will have false starts and slips!

This inevitably happens, because like most mortals, we let down our efforts to maintain a spiritual focus. We all have to learn by our own experience that

"...we must carry the vision of God's will into all of our activities. ...These are thoughts which must be constantly with us" (*AA*, 84).

Sobriety doesn't come from abstaining from our drug of choice. Sobriety comes from growing in our awareness of the goodness of God (Mormon 1:15) and the fact that He "is doing for us what we could not do for ourselves" (*AA*, 84).

Application:

Turn to **Moroni 4:3** and **Moroni 5:2**. Prayerfully read and ponder the phrases in the Sacrament prayers that express our covenant with the Lord to **"always remember Him."** Write about what the Sacrament has meant to you at different times in your life. What does it mean now? What is your level of willingness to forgive yourself and to *practice* always remembering your Savior?

4.5 Alma 7:23—I would that ye should be humble, and be submissive and gentle; easy to be entreated; full of patience and long-suffering...

We often think of God entreating us to be full of patience and long-suffering towards other people, but have we ever given much thought to the idea of God pleading with us to have patience and long-suffering towards Him?

Patience and longsuffering are very closely related to giving the other person the benefit of the doubt. It's synonymous with trusting someone.

The verse continues:

> **...asking for whatsoever things ye stand in need, both spiritual and temporal; always returning thanks unto God for whatsoever things ye do receive.**

This is a perfect description of those who are willing to leave their lives (and the lives of others) in God's hands. The ultimate working relationship with God, as well as with another person, is to be able to own our own voice and express our truth. This truth includes expressing **"whatsoever** [we] **stand in need"** to express. Sometimes we just need to *say it*.

And then we must be willing to let go of the results and receive, with a positive heart, what they (the other person or God) are willing or able to supply.

Application:

Ponder and prayerfully write about your feelings towards God, after realizing His human (immortal and exalted though He may be) desire for our understanding and patience with Him and His purposes.

An old television show began with the hero making this statement, "Trust me, I know what I'm doing." Write about whether or not you are willing to believe that God knows what He's doing. Is your level of willingness to trust God increasing?

4.6 2 Nephi 9:23—Having perfect faith in the Holy One of Israel.

We often hear advice such as, "You need to have more faith in yourself." No. It is not faith in ourselves that brings us the peace and serenity we crave. It is accepting and trusting God's benevolence in all things that will bring us along the path to perfect faith. With faith in God, we can move through the events of our lives with greater calmness and cheerfulness.

Application:

Ponder and prayerfully write about your past experiences with having faith in yourself. Why do you think believing in yourself needs to come only after you have learned to depend on your Savior? Write about the Savior's statement:

> **I am the vine, ye *are* the branches: He that abideth in me, and I in him, the same bringeth forth much fruit: for without me ye can do nothing (John 15:5; emphasis original).**

How does this statement encourage us to rely on God as our source of power?

4.7 3 Nephi 27:13—This is the gospel which I have given unto you—that I came into the world to do the will of my Father, because my Father sent me.

Have you ever wished that someone would sum up the whole gospel in one statement? Well, someone has. Or should I say, *Someone* has.

In this verse, Christ summarizes the secret of living a miraculous, gifted life—a life in which we are filled with a sense of fulfillment and oneness with God and with all that are His: Do the will of God.

The entire Gospel of Jesus Christ can also be summed up in this Step Three motto: "God can. And He will... *if we let Him.*" Christ lived the principle we call Step Three to perfection. By making the decision to take the Third Step, we follow His example, His path.

Application:

Christ lived the path of not just Step Three, but One and Two also.

Read **John 5:30; 8:28** (Step One) and **Matthew 6:13** (Step Two). Ponder and write about the idea that God is not asking us to do something that He Himself has not already modeled for us.

Supplemental Scriptures for Step Three

The following are additional scriptures which support Step Three:

2 Nephi 4:32–34 Nephi expresses to the Lord his desire for help with his weaknesses, then states his complete trust in God to regulate and orchestrate his life.

2 Nephi 8:7—The people in whose heart I have written my law. Self-will avails us nothing; it is God's will that we must have written upon our hearts.

2 Nephi 31:19—For ye have not come thus far save it were by the word of Christ with unshaken faith in him. Trusting the Lord in all things is the exact equivalent of having "unshaken faith in him," knowing that He has enough power to save all who desire salvation.

Jacob 2:18–19—But before ye seek for riches, seek ye for the kingdom of God. And after ye have obtained a hope in Christ ye shall obtain riches, if ye seek them. This truth taught in the Book of Mormon illustrates the same basic sequence as the Twelve Steps—seek God first, then other blessings follow.

Jacob 5:21–23 The Lord knows best how to nourish us. We can trust Him to give us what we need.

Alma 26:15—We have been instruments in his hands. Coming out of the darkness of this life means awakening from the insanity of "self-will run riot" (*AA*, 62) and learning to relax into the role of instrument rather than surgeon, of player rather than director.

Alma 34:32—This life is the time for men to prepare to meet God. The preparation we need, which will enable us to meet Him in this life as well as the next, is to turn our will and lives over to Him.

Alma 37:6—By small and simple things are great things brought to pass. Such a small and simple thing, to make the decision to turn our will and our lives over to the care of God, but it offers great rewards. Keeping it simple is a Twelve Step key.

Alma 48:15–16—This was their faith, that…God would prosper them…warn them to flee, or to prepare for war… that God would made it known unto them whither they should go. These people, under the leadership of Moroni, had turned their lives and will over to the care of God. God, in turn, cared for them. Whether battling invading armies, or the armies of our addictions, God can and will direct us in all things.

Alma 57:27—Now this was the faith of these whom I have spoken; they are young, and their minds are firm, and they do put their trust in God continually. The stripling warriors were protected from harm and were victorious over their enemies. Helaman attributes this to their faith and continuous trust in God.

Alma 61:12–13—We would subject ourselves…if he should command us so to do. But behold he doth not… but that we should put our trust in him. If we are willing to do anything the Lord requires (turn our will and our life over to God), He will deliver us from our enemies (character weaknesses).

Helaman 5:12—It is upon the rock of our Redeemer, who is Christ, the Son of God, that ye must build your foundation…[the storm] shall have no power over you. The sure foundation of Jesus Christ enables us to withstand the most severe trials. Temptation has no power over us when we turn our lives and our wills over to Him and are receiving His instructions to us personally.

Helaman 7:5 A negative example of people who follow their own will. When we perform according to our own will, the result is (only) worldly gain and sin.

Helaman 12:6—They do not desire that the Lord... should rule and reign over them...they do set at naught his counsels, and they will not that he should be their guide. Once we know the will of the Lord, not doing it is an act of choice on our part. We set at "naught" (to regard or treat as of no importance) His counsel, and use our will to choose not to let the Lord be our guide.

3 Nephi 14:21—Not every one that saith unto me, Lord, Lord, shall enter into the kingdom of heaven; but he that *doeth the will* of my Father who is in heaven (emphasis added). Everyone will eventually recognize Christ as the ultimate Higher Power. Recognition alone, however, does not demonstrate our oneness with Him. Oneness with Him is demonstrated by our willingness to do His will.

4 Nephi 1:15—There was no contention in the land, because of the love of God which did dwell in the hearts of the people. These people were filled with the love of God first, then were taught by that love relationship how to avoid contention and to live peaceably with one another **(Moroni 7:3)**. They learned, as President Benson advised us, to put God before everyone else in their lives (see *Ensign*, May 1988, 4).

Mormon 5:23—Know ye not that ye are in the hands of God? Sometimes we are afraid to put our lives into the hands of God, because we have not yet learned to trust Him. As we practice this trust, we come to realize that we are in loving hands and that He uses His power for our good **(Alma 26:35)**.

Ether 6:4—Commending themselves unto the Lord their God. The Jaredites trusted the Lord to carry them through the depths of the sea to a new land. How fearful they must have been tempted to be. No matter how fearful the circumstances we face, we can entrust our very lives to the Lord for safekeeping.

Ether 9:35—And it came to pass that when they had *humbled themselves* sufficiently...the Lord did show forth his power unto them in preserving them" (emphasis added). Humility is not forced upon us. Becoming humble is a decision we make. It is only after we become humble that the Lord is able to show forth His mighty power unto our salvation.

Ether 12:6—Ye receive no witness until after the trial of your faith. The trial of our faith is whether we will decide to reconcile ourselves to the will of God and trust Him in all things.

Ether 15:34—Whether the Lord will...that I suffer the will of the Lord in the flesh, it mattereth not. These are the last words recorded by Ether, as he ended his record of the Jaredites. He is an example of a person who has truly given his will and his life to God.

Moroni 10:32—Yea, come unto Christ, and be perfected in him...and love God with all your might, mind and strength, then is his grace sufficient for you. To be "perfected in Christ" is to surrender our will to His will, and to the will of the Father **(3 Nephi 27:13)**.

Other References for Step Three

As you find other references to Step Three in your personal daily scripture study, list them here:

Step Four

Made a searching and fearless moral inventory of ourselves. Made a searching and fearless written inventory of our past in order to thoroughly examine ourselves as to our pride and other weaknesses with the intent of recognizing our own carnal state and our need for Christ's Atonement.

Step Five

Admitted to God, to ourselves, and to another human being the exact nature of our wrongs. Honestly shared this inventory with God and with another person, thus demonstrating the sincerity of our repentance, and our willingness to give away all our sins that we might know Him.

Two Reasons You're a Hero

Do you know how much courage it takes to open this chapter on Steps Four and Five?! You're a hero if you can even read this introduction! Why would I say something so exclamatory? Two reasons.

First, Steps Four and Five are one of those places where "self-will may slam [the door to our willingness] shut again" (*12&12*, 35). In fact, it's so common in Twelve

Step programs for people to either stall out on Steps Four and Five, leap-frog over them, or skitter across them like a water bug, barely breaking the surface, that it's almost a joke. It's a nervous and half-hearted joke, though, because everyone senses the truth—the path to complete healing lies through Steps Four and Five. They are as essential as Steps One, Two, and Three.

Looking at our past to acknowledge the good, face the painful, and come to an honest peace with our life is a natural and necessary continuation of the first three steps. Taking Steps Four and Five confirms and sustains the faith that began as a desire to change. It is the action that supports the decision made in Step Three, to turn our life over to the care of God.

Second, you're a hero—even a "savior on Mount Zion"—according to LDS therapist, Carlfred Broderick:

> My experience in various church callings and in my profession as a family therapist has convinced me that God actively intervenes in some destructive lineages, assigning a valiant spirit to break the chain of destructiveness in such families. Although these children may suffer innocently as victims of violence, neglect, and exploitation, through the grace of God some find the strength to "metabolize" the poison within themselves, refusing to pass it on to future generations. Before them were generations of destructive pain; after them the line flows clear and pure... In suffering innocently that others might not suffer, such persons, in some degree, become as "saviors on Mount Zion" by

> helping to bring salvation to a lineage (Carlfred Broderick, "I Have a Question," *Ensign*, Aug. 1986, 38).

By facing and acknowledging our weaknesses, we can be almost certain that we are facing and acknowledging the same tendencies our parents and progenitors struggled with in one manifestation or another. The miracle of one individual embracing the "mighty change" and accepting the redeeming power of the Atonement of Jesus Christ is that it creates change in an entire family line. So, let's gird up our loins and rise to the challenge of Steps Four and Five!

The process begins by taking a minute to review and strap on the spiritual armor available to us in Steps One through Three. In these steps we have begun to face some humbling truths about life and our relationship to it: we can't control life; we can't make it go the way we want it to go. In Step Three we decided to turn our will and our lives over to God and practice trusting that, somehow, everything happens for a benevolent purpose.

Most of us long to find this place of peace with God and His will, but we are confused about how to do it. We are either terrified to look into our past, or we are in such denial that we minimize it and brush it off as not worth remembering. Some of us just plain don't have memories. Whatever our feelings, the unavoidable fact is that the path to the healing and peace that we so desperately need and want, is through the depths of humility that Steps Four and Five represent.

> We pocket our pride and go to it, illuminating every twist of character, every dark cranny of the past. Once we have

> taken [Steps Four and Five], withholding nothing, [we will find these results, obtain these blessings]…
>
> - We will be delighted.
> - We can look the world [everyone else] in the eye.
> - We can be alone at perfect peace and ease [the opposite condition from dis-ease].
> - Our fears fall from us.
> - We begin to feel the nearness of our Creator.
>
> We may have had certain spiritual beliefs [a testimony of the Lord and His church], but now we begin to have a spiritual experience (*AA*, p. 75).

Step Four: Looking for More Than Symptoms

Most people stand on the threshold of Step Four, staring into the foggy, and often intentionally forgotten, depths of their past. You may find yourself reacting like this: "A fearless and thorough inventory? How can you expect me to look at my past like that? Obviously, you have no idea how many sad and foolish things I've done. You have no idea how much sorrow, pain, loss, loneliness, misunderstanding, regret, and resentment I have buried.

I can't imagine dredging all that up. I can barely live with it repressed. Facing it head-on would kill me, or at least push me off the deep end. This program promised that God would restore me to sanity, not require me to give up what little I've worked so hard to maintain."

If this is your reaction, let me reassure you that Step Four is terrifying for most of us, until we work it. I can assure you that those of us who have taken this step are still alive and intact—mentally, emotionally and spiritually. In fact, we are healthier in every way than when we carried such burdens. We have come to realize that acting out our addictive behaviors was just a symptom:

> Our [addictive behavior] was but a symptom... We had to get down to causes and conditions... Therefore we started upon a personal inventory... we searched out the flaws in our make-up which [contributed] to our [hard times] (*AA*, 64).

Step Four picks up where Three left off. It answers the question, "*How* do I turn my will and life over to God?" The first three steps help us come to believe, "I can't; God can; I think I'll let Him." Steps Four and Five teach us, "I never could; God always could; in fact, He already has."

As we work through Step Four, we realize that during the hardest times, even in our most lost and fallen moments, we are still participating in God's benevolent plan for the progress and growth of all His children. Doing the fearless and searching inventory required in Step Four is one way in which we turn our lives over to God.

Do a Life Review? Why Not Just "Drive On"?

On the other hand, you may be having the alternate reaction: "Do a life review? What's the point in that? Sure, there were a few painful moments, but isn't that the way life is for all of us? I want to fix myself here and now and drive on, not looking back. That's what feels right for me. I don't have anything to inventory… do I?"

Social science research, as well as personal experience, has shown that those who minimize or reject their past are hurting just as much as those who can't stop thinking about it. Those who have genuinely healthy attitudes about their life can remember the past, talk about it, and acknowledge both their positive and negative experiences and relationships. Step Four is the doorway to resolution and integrity about our life experiences.

At this point, this inventory, this review of our experiences, feelings and lessons, is between each one of us and the Lord. Step Four is not about sharing with anyone else. It is a private interlude. Taking this step is like stepping into a sound-proof booth and sharing our secrets with the Lord, who loves us unconditionally and whose mercy can satisfy justice. We find upon taking a prayerful Step Four, asking the Lord to reveal His perspective to us on our lives, that we are often overwhelmed with tenderness and empathy from God, even as the worst moments of our lives are reviewed.

A fourth step is an amazing revelation of God's love and mercy, far more than of His judgment. It is the living experience of His testimony in **John 12:47: "I came not to judge…but to save."** By the time we finish our first four steps, most of us have learned to appreciate the process that turns sorrowful choices into well-internalized lessons.

> As we persist, a brand-new kind of confidence is born, and the sense of relief at finally facing ourselves is indescribable. These are the first fruits of Step Four (*12&12*, 50).

That is the power of Step Four, its gift to us. It helps us see the patterns of our past actions *and* the patterns of our past beliefs. We did what we did because we believed what we believed. Those beliefs were often based on fear and distrust, anger and pain. While we can't turn the clock back and change our past, we *can* change our beliefs—and that will change our present and future lives.

Beliefs can be changed, even if all we have is a desire to believe differently. But changing our beliefs involves the process Alma outlined: first, we have to desire to change; next, we must believe that we can; then, we exercise faith in Christ and take action **(Alma 32:27)**. The result of this process? We *will* be changed and we will know that Christ is there for each of us individually.

Step Five: Being Stripped of Pride by Coming Clean

It has been said that the Twelve Steps "ask us to go contrary to our natural desires" (*12&12*, 55). If this is so, then they are exactly the prescription for putting off the natural man and ceasing to be an enemy to God **(Mosiah 3:19)**.

> They [all twelve steps] deflate our egos. When it comes to ego deflation, few Steps are harder to take than Five. But [none] is

> more necessary to longtime...peace of mind than this one (*12&12*, 55).

Why? Because it strips us of pride—and this stripping of pride is absolutely necessary for a spiritual life.

> **Behold, are ye stripped of pride?... if ye are not ye are not prepared to meet God (Alma 5:28).**

Humility is the essence of Step Five. Our humility is not complete until we are willing to let someone else, besides God, know us thoroughly and honestly. Our goal is to leave no stone unturned, no unexposed place where the Liar (Satan) can hide. We want all the cancer out. It might help to think of Step Four as an MRI or ultrasound, and Step Five as radiation or chemotherapy.

In Twelve Step programs there is a saying: "We're only as sick as we are secret." We are beings of light and truth **(D&C 93:29)**, and as such, we cannot be mentally and emotionally whole and healed while keeping secrets.

Any hidden thing of darkness, kept secret within us, brings us spiritual dis-ease (lack of peace). We toss and turn in our pain, unable to find rest to our souls. We are like the princess and the pea, but instead of lying upon piles of mattresses, we stack piles of compulsive addictive behaviors between us and the dark truths from which we are hiding. We desperately pretend they never happened.

But it doesn't work. We are of royal birth, spiritually, and our sensitivity to sin is that of a celestial being who has fallen into a thorny bed of lies—false beliefs about ourselves, about God, and about life. These lies cause us soul-deep pain. Step Five provides the path to wholeness and recovery of our former innocence.

However, recognizing our character weaknesses and the unrighteous actions they have led us to take is not enough. Acknowledging these things privately to God is not enough. Only when we are willing to bear witness to another person of the exact nature of our need for Christ's Atonement, are we ready to come to peace with our past, to forgive it, and to let it be. Nothing restores our mental and emotional well-being like the feeling of innocence we gain when we have nothing left to hide.

What are the mechanics of taking Step Five? Armed with the written inventory we made in Step Four, listing both the mistakes we've made against others and the mistakes others have made against us, we make an appointment with a Twelve Step sponsor. Or we visit with a trusted friend, or possibly with our bishop, if there are things in our inventory that need confession to a bishop. Make the selection of whom to share your inventory with a matter of prayer and fasting.

Ask for at least an hour of time. You're worth it. Take your written inventory. Read it all. Get it out. Clean house. If the person you're sharing your inventory with is not familiar with Twelve Step program, you may want to warn them that some of your inventory may seem silly and trivial, but you are trying to search out *everything* for which you feel guilty, ashamed, angry, or resentful. Even if it is just a childhood incident that still lingers in your memory, it's on your list. Explain that you want to relate this inventory with absolute honesty, leaving no stone unturned. You want to be free of any excuse for guilt or resentment, because those are the things that are blocking your ability to receive the Spirit fully and to wholeheartedly feel the cleansing power of the Savior's Atonement.

Prayerful study of the following scriptures and completion of the suggested writing exercises will help to internalize the eternal principles represented in Steps Four and Five. God bless you in this most amazing journey of recovery. We who have lived through these steps promise you a sense of relief and freedom like you never thought you could have again in this life.

Steps Four & Five—Week One

1.1 2 Nephi 9:33—Wo unto the uncircumcised of heart, for a knowledge of their iniquities shall smite them at the last day.

In the discussion of Principle Four in *He Did Deliver Me from Bondage,* I used the symbolism of the uncircumcised heart, suggesting that we must reveal our life to the Lord, holding nothing back from Him, not even our most private thoughts and feelings.

An uncircumcised heart is still hidden beneath layers of shame and pride. In its hidden and unexposed condition, this heart is infected with fear, anger, resentment, guilt, and other negative attributes. A heart in this condition is often numb, unable to sense and receive the whisperings of the Spirit. To circumcise it we must cut through our facades and pretenses, and reveal our innermost self. Even though this procedure is embarrassing and painful, it will be the wisest and best thing we ever do.

Application:

Ponder and prayerfully write about some of the facades and pretenses you use as smokescreens to hide your real feelings. How much do you deny, even to yourself? List the regrets, sorrows, griefs, angers, frustrations, and feelings of self-pity you keep to yourself.

Don't make the mistake of skipping the writing part of the Fourth Step. Writing out your inventory is essential to making it thorough:

> In dealing with resentments, we set them on paper.…We reviewed our fears thoroughly. We put them on paper (*AA*, 64, 68).
>
> Therefore, thoroughness ought to be the watchword when taking inventory. In this connection, it is wise to write… It will be an aid to clear thinking and honest appraisal. It will be the first *tangible* evidence of our complete willingness to move forward (*12&12*, 54; emphasis original).

1.2 2 Nephi 9:45-46—Turn away from your sins; shake off the chains of him that would bind you fast; come unto that God who is the rock of your salvation. Prepare your souls for that glorious day…that ye may not remember your awful guilt in perfectness, and be constrained to exclaim: Holy, holy are thy judgments, O Lord God Almighty—but I know my guilt; I transgressed thy law, and my transgressions are mine; and the devil hath obtained me, that I am a prey to his awful misery.

> The devil has no power over us only as we permit him. The moment we revolt at anything which comes from God, the devil

> takes power (*Teachings of the Prophet Joseph Smith*, 181).

In the light of the Prophet Joseph's words, I find it understandable why Nephi would invite us to simply **"shake off the chains"** of the adversary. While the Liar may fashion chains of lies over our lifetime, he cannot fasten them upon us. We may be weighted down with such chains, but we are not locked into them. Shaking them off may take some time, it is true. Being **"flaxen" (2 Nephi 26:22)** as they are, it can be a bit like trying to shake off cobwebs. But it can be done.

Doing a Fourth Step is about being ready to face the whole truth—*now*. It is about being willing to own our accountability—*now*. We look for the character traits in ourselves that keep us from letting go of poor choices in our past, whether those choices were made by ourselves or by others.

> If my disturbance was seemingly caused by the behavior of [another], why do I lack the ability to accept conditions I cannot change? (*12&12*, 52).

There is no other way we can become **"prepared to meet God"** than to do this accounting while yet in this life **(Alma 34:32)**.

Application:

Prayerfully ponder and write about the idea that "my transgressions are mine." Are you willing to stop focusing on the indiscretions, ignorance, mistakes, foolish, or malicious choices of others, and to look at your own instead?

1.3 Alma 12:10—And therefore, he that will harden his heart, the same receiveth the lesser portion of the word; and he that will not harden his heart, to him is given the greater portion of the word, until it is given unto him to know the mysteries of God until he know them in full.

God does not shut us out or withhold His words from us. We are the ones who turn away from Him. We stop seeking His gifts of counsel and comfort through the gift of the Holy Ghost. By keeping our secrets, we are contributing to the hardheartedness that Step Four is designed to soften.

When we contemplate doing the fourth step, fear and unbelief flare up to stop us from taking this amazing opportunity. Pride rears its head—either head-on, as in, "My life's not *that* bad. I've cleared up all the bad things with the bishop," or in reverse, "My life is so bad, I couldn't possibly take a close look at it." We do not need to shrink from this step. The Lord will lead us and give us His counsel and comfort during this inventory work. He will not leave us alone with it. It will become one of the greatest spiritual experiences we could ever hope to have.

Application:

Ponder and prayerfully write about your feelings concerning doing this inventory. Picture yourself doing what **Moroni 10:32** suggests—coming to Christ *before* you **"deny** [yourself] **of all ungodliness."** Write about the success or lack of success you've had keeping your sins and your shame to yourself. Does this course of action make you feel better or worse?

1.4 Alma 11:43-44—The spirit and the body shall be reunited again… even as we now are at this time; and we shall be brought to stand before God, knowing even as we know now, and have a bright recollection of all our guilt. Now, this restoration shall come to all, both old and young, both bond and free, both male and female, both the wicked and the righteous.

Often when we come to Step Four, we are put off by the idea of looking back over our past with such scrutiny. We are tempted to think this somehow violates the concept taught in the gospel of our sins being forgotten and becoming **"white as snow" (Isaiah 1:18)**. Yet, here in this verse is the testimony that a **"restoration"** to a **"bright recollection"** of all our unexamined and unsurrendered sins will come to all of us—old, young, bond, free, male, female, wicked or righteous.

Application:

We are all promised a **"bright recollection"** of our guilt at some point. Prayerfully ponder and write about why it might be good to deliberately and consciously choose to examine and inventory *any* sins (thoughts, words, or deeds that diminish our closeness and consciousness of God) that may still remain in our lives.

Look closely at those sins hiding behind the rationale of, "That's too little to matter," or lurking behind the lie, "That's too big to deal with." Do you have any of either of these types of memories? Why put off this day of searching and fearless inventory?

1.5 Alma 10:6—Nevertheless, I did harden my heart, for I was called many times and I would not hear; therefore I knew concerning these things, yet I would not know; therefore I went on rebelling against God.

The words of Amulek are so revelatory. In the preceding two verses (4 and 5), we have the definite impression that he is a stable and steady man, with an accumulation of wealth. He is a sober man, a decent, upstanding member of his community. We can also surmise that he is most likely an active member of the church.

According to his own testimony, he has watched the workings of the Lord with **"this people."** But, through all that, he has not had a personal, internal, heart-deep conversion to God. He has felt enticed, but has not chosen to hear.

> Because our surface record hasn't looked too bad, we have frequently been abashed to find [upon looking deeper into our character] that this is so simply because we have buried these selfsame defects deep down

> in us under thick layers of self-justification (*12&12*, 53–54).

Application:

Prayerfully ponder and write concerning this very real phenomenon of denial, or dissociation, from a reality we aren't ready to face. What better definition could we find for denial than, **"I knew concerning these things, yet I would not know"**?

Denial and dissociation are the biggest obstacles in approaching Step Four. Amulek refers to this condition as a hardened heart. A heart that is hardened against God (resistant to the whole truth) cannot hear His word (perceive truth—negative or positive).

What reality in your past, present or future are you resisting or pretending didn't happen? Or isn't happening, even now? Or isn't going to happen eventually?

1.6 2 Nephi 9:34—Wo unto the liar, for he shall be thrust down to hell.

A person who lives a lie, a pretense, doesn't have to wait for the last judgment to be **"thrust down to hell."** Such a person lives in a hell here and now—a hell of isolation with no rest or peace. Lies and shameful secrets are the means by which the adversary creates invisible walls between people. How can someone who is harboring a lie and living in a fog of untruth have peace?

As a child of the **"Father of lights" (James 1:17)**, your truest nature is not that of **"the natural man" (Mosiah 3:19)** or an enemy to God. We become an enemy to God in direct proportion to how deeply we believe the lies we have inherited from the significant others in our lives, who in turn inherited lies from their significant others. If we are to repent and avoid passing these same lies on to our children, we must get in conscious contact with them and present them to the Lord for removal (Steps Six and Seven).

One of the greatest and most miraculous effects of taking Step Five by sharing our inventory with another person, is that our sense of isolation and loneliness is almost instantly taken away.

> What are we likely to receive from Step Five? For one thing, we shall get rid of that terrible sense of isolation we've always had. Almost without exception, [people with addictive tendencies] are tortured by loneliness. Even before [we developed our addictive behaviors], nearly all of us suffered the feeling that we didn't quite belong (*12&12*, 57).

Application:

Ponder and write about how you have sold your birthright as a child of light to the adversary of truth, even to Satan, the father of lies. Write about why he is also called "the spoiler."

How do you see that you and your loved ones have been in bondage to this father of lies? How has his influence enticed you to forget your true identity? Write about your desire to eliminate his influence from your life, to reveal the lies that have spoiled so much of your family's past happiness and potential.

1.7 Moroni 10:22—And if ye have no hope ye must needs be in despair; and despair cometh because of iniquity.

So many of us live what has been coined as "lives of quiet desperation." The word "despair" works in that statement, too. Some of us react to despair by saying, "What the heck," and raising havoc all around us. Others of us stuff the despair, holding it at bay by being as outwardly active in "good works" as possible.

The truth is, if we feel a sense of despair, we can be sure that iniquity lies at the root of it, somewhere. Somewhere inside, there are wounds that we've either given or received that have not been acknowledged (Steps Four and Five) or resolved (Steps Six and Seven).

Application:

One of the simplest forms of a first-time written inventory is to just take a piece of paper and divide it in half. On one side write, "Times I've hurt others," and on the other side write, "Times I've been hurt by others." Then, write short phrases to represent each incident you can remember. Are you ready to take this simple inventory now? If so, go ahead and do it.

If not, write about why you're not ready. What will it take for you to become ready?

Steps Four & Five—Week Two

2.1 Alma 42:30—Do not endeavor to excuse yourself in the least point because of your sins, by denying the justice of God; but do you let the justice of God, and his mercy, and his long-suffering have full sway in your heart; and let it bring you down to the dust in humility.

Doing a *fearless* and *thorough* moral inventory is in perfect harmony with this verse. As we do our fourth step, we work on letting go of excusing ourselves **"in the least point."** We come out of denial about three things: (1) how much we have done to hurt others; (2) how much we have been hurt by others; and especially, (3) how much we've hurt ourselves.

It is vital, as we do this thorough housecleaning, to notice that this verse calls for justice, followed by a double dose of kindness in the form of mercy and long-suffering. We must allow this kindness to take over our heart, to **"have full sway."** Then we will have the courage to be fearless and thorough.

> "But how can I be kind to them, considering what they've done to hurt me?" Or maybe our cry is, "How can I ever be kind to myself, considering the stupid things I've done?" Either way, the promise of working through Twelve Step based recovery is that,

> "God will show us how to take a kindly and tolerant view of each and every one" (*AA*, 67).

Application:

Look up "justice," "mercy" and "long-suffering" in the dictionary. Copy the definitions into your journal. Prayerfully write about how God's mercy and long-suffering always accompany any justice we may have to face. What do you think the scriptures mean when they say that while mercy cannot rob justice, it can *satisfy* justice **(Alma 42:25; Alma 34:16)**?

2.2 2 Nephi 4:17-18

Nephi admits a portion of his inventory. He allows us to see that even though he was a great prophet, he had reason to wrestle with shame and guilt. We too will be **"encompassed about"** by our temptations and sins unless we face them as squarely and honestly as Nephi did. Nephi states that we don't have to **"give way to temptations" (v. 27)**. We can follow Nephi's example and make a searching and fearless inventory of our inner selves and motives.

This business of inventory seems painful at first, because, when we start, we are usually looking for the bad things we've *done*—the embarrassing, shameful actions we've engaged in and spent our lifetime trying to hide (thus never being able to forget them).

As we get into the inventory process, though, we are surprised to find how gently the Spirit of the Lord encircles us while we take a close, honest look at our lives. We find that He is far more interested in our motives, our beliefs and our erroneous rationalizations than with the actions themselves. He is much more interested in us getting down to the "root causes" (*12&12*, 53) that still contribute to our current lack of peace.

Application:

Try an inventory practice run by prayerfully pondering and asking the Lord to help you do a heart-deep (beliefs and motives, thoughts and feelings) inventory of *one* time you did something about which you still feel guilty or ashamed.

2.3 3 Nephi 12:22, 28

In these two verses, the Lord Himself plainly reveals that it is what goes on in our hearts, in the private secret places of our lives, that matters. Hoarding our secrets may help us to avoid public discipline for a time, but they will not fool God. We are deceived if we think that outward actions of piety or industry can cover hearts filled with anger and discontent.

Application:

Prayerfully ponder and write about whether or not avoiding the outward penalties of society is a sufficient standard for a disciple of Christ. Write about a time in your life when you might have been covering inner turmoil by outward appearances.

2.4 2 Nephi 9:14—We shall have a perfect knowledge of all our guilt, and our uncleanness, and our nakedness; and the righteous shall have a perfect knowledge of their enjoyment, and their righteousness, being clothed with purity, yea, even with the robe of righteousness.

Have you ever thought about the fact that since there is not *one* of us who is totally guilty or perfectly pure, both sides of this pronouncement will be answered on our heads? We are all, *simultaneously,* in both camps. There will come a time when we will each have a perfect knowledge of our guilt *and* a perfect knowledge of our enjoyment and right choices.

Application:

The fourth step inventory process does not mean we must focus only on the negatives in our past. It means that we are ready to be totally honest—*wholly honest*—and allow the Spirit of Truth to remind us and restore to us both our enjoyment and our guilt. We are willing to be brought to as perfect, or complete, a knowledge as we are able to understand.

Practice doing a fourth step inventory by taking a recent day—yesterday or one day in the past week—and listing (in brief phrases) both the negatives and the positives. Count your blessings, but also admit your challenges—both are part of the reality of life.

2.5 Mosiah 26:29—If he confess his sins before thee and me, and repenteth in the sincerity of his heart.

Many people wonder why the fifth step has to include "another human being," and wish that it required confession to God only. Listen to the harmony between the following quote and the scripture just cited:

> Until we actually sit down and talk aloud about what we have so long hidden, our willingness to clean house is still largely theoretical (*12&12*, 60).

Application:

Prayerfully meditate on this image of a house that needs cleaning. Write a description of the house, picturing different rooms to represent different parts of your life story. Maybe you have an attic that is scary and full of shadows and unopened boxes. Maybe it's a basement. Or a back room. Or maybe a whole back wing of your house. Maybe you've been able to keep every room looking presentable, but you wouldn't dare let them see in the closets or under the bed.

That's the metaphor. See where you can go with it by writing about what needs to be done to clean up the hidden areas so that it can be lived in and enjoyed.

Write about seeing your sponsor and/or priesthood leader as someone who, by listening, is going to help you open up, clean up, and remodel.

2.6 Mosiah 26:35–36—And whosoever repented of their sins and did confess them, them he did number among the people of the church; and those that would not confess their sins and repent of their iniquity, the same were not numbered among the people of the church.

This is about actual church discipline, but let's think for a minute about the feelings in your own heart of not belonging, not fitting in, not being **"numbered among the people of the church."** In exercise 1.6, we addressed the often gnawing, chronic feeling of loneliness that torments people who resort to addictive behaviors. Doing a fourth step inventory, and "giving it away" in a fifth step, is such a powerful experience in breaking free of that feeling.

> When we...for the first time in our lives stood among people who seemed to understand [this chronic loneliness], the sense of belonging was tremendously exciting... Until we had talked with complete candor... and had listened to someone else do the same thing, we still didn't belong. Step Five was the answer. It was the beginning of true kinship with man and God (*12&12*, 57).

Application:

Prayerfully ponder and write about a part of your life that you avoid talking about, that causes you to feel separate, different or isolated from other members of the church. Even though you may go to church and hold positions, you may still feel like you're a stranger and that no one really knows you. Write about whether you've faced these feelings at any time in your past. Are you facing some of them now? Describe and reflect on how that feels.

2.7 Jacob 4:3—Now in this thing we do rejoice; and we labor diligently to engraven these words upon plates, hoping that our beloved brethren and our children will receive them with thankful hearts, and look upon them that they may learn with joy and not with sorrow, neither with contempt, concerning their first parents.

One of the biggest hindrances to doing a fourth step is that we are terrified that someone is going to come across our record, read it and have contempt or sorrow or shock at our life's complete story—woven through with the frailties and weaknesses and foolish, immature choices we've made. It's hard to believe that anyone might ever receive our plainness and honesty with thankful hearts.

Application:

What would it be like to come across one of your grandparents' or great-grandparents' journals and find that it contained only the positive parts of their life experiences—no mention of personal moments of challenge or weakness, temptations, poor choices, or repentance processes? Would you feel disappointed? Surprised?

Write about what we can learn from seeing others successfully face and overcome being mortal. What are the very best lessons we can record for those who come after us?

Steps Four & Five—Week Three

3.1 Alma 18:32—And Ammon said: Yea, and he looketh down upon all the children of men; and he knows all the thoughts and intents of the heart; for by his hand were they all created from the beginning.

Often, when thinking of the inventory process, we are terrified of reviewing *what* we have done. But the Lord knows the **"thoughts and intents of the heart."** He knew all of us, as we were each created from the beginning, when we were innocent spirit children with our Heavenly Father.

The Lord knows the "whys" of our misdeeds, too. He knows the foolish, childish, immature choices we have made. He knows what it is like to know the gospel with your mind, but not have it deeply internalized into your heart. He knows what it is like to be you, in your shoes. He experienced your life in the Garden of Gethsemane.

Application:

Prayerfully ponder how Step Three—turning your will and life over to God—is acted upon in Step Four by taking a personal inventory. Write about "How turning my life over to God means surrendering my past—mistakes and all."

How could taking Steps Four and Five actually carry out the Third Step prayer that begins, "God, I offer myself to Thee…" (*AA*, 63)?

3.2 Alma 39:7-8—I would not dwell upon your crimes, to harrow up your soul, if it were not for your good. But behold, ye cannot hide your crimes from God; and except ye repent they will stand as a testimony against you at the last day.

The hard things we have to do, including a fifth step, are all for benevolent reasons. Neither our Heavenly Father nor the Lord wants to make us suffer for our sins.

Suffering comes from trying to hide our sins, not from doing what has to be done to confess them and genuinely forsake them. Taking the fourth and the fifth steps is not only "a clear recognition of what and who we really are," but also "a sincere attempt to become what we could be" (*12&12*, 58).

Application:

Ponder and prayerfully write about how it isn't just at "the last day" that our sins will stand as a testimony against us.

Write about how our sins "stand against" us even now, each day of our lives by keeping us from "a clear recognition of what and who we really are."

How do they keep us from making "a sincere attempt to become what we could be."

3.3 Moroni 10:4-5—And when ye shall receive these things, I would exhort you that ye would ask God, the Eternal Father, in the name of Christ, if these things are not true; and if ye shall ask with a sincere heart, with real intent, having faith in Christ, he will manifest the truth of it unto you, by the power of the Holy Ghost. And by the power of the Holy Ghost ye may know the truth of all things.

A personal inventory is not something you have to do alone. The Holy Ghost, also known as the Comforter, will be with you every step of the way. He will convey to you the cleansing counsel and amazing comfort of the Savior's own words **(2 Nephi 32:3)**.

Remember that this is the same Jesus who had mercy on the woman taken in adultery, who was not afraid to touch lepers, or to eat with outcasts. This is the same Jesus who talked to the Samaritan woman honestly but tenderly and healed a man's child, even though that man couldn't honestly say that his belief was perfect **(Mark 9:24)**.

To know the truth about ourselves, we use the same process as knowing any other truth. We pray with **"a sincere heart, with real intent, having faith in Christ,"** knowing that He is merciful beyond our greatest hopes. The Holy Ghost will introduce us to Christ—the second and greatest comforter of all. The Holy Ghost is our witness of truth.

Application:

As you internalize Step Four—the principle of heart-deep honesty and humility—prayerfully ponder and write your thoughts about the exchange of opening your whole life to the Lord in order to have Him open His life and His mercy and power (grace) to you. Prayerfully listen and record His own words of comfort and counsel to you—His light unto your understanding—in your own language **(2 Nephi 31:3)**.

3.4 3 Nephi 17:14—Jesus groaned within himself, and said: Father, I am troubled because of the wickedness of the people of the house of Israel.

In exactly the same way, His Spirit, the Light of Christ that exists in each of us without exception, is troubled by wickedness. It is because of His Light which each of us bear at the center of our hearts, that we are troubled by wickedness—both our own and also that which we have experienced at the hands of others. We are beings of light and truth. Thus even the smallest hidden act of darkness, harbored within our souls, torments and sickens us spiritually, emotionally and even physically. Doing an inventory is the beginning of the end of that torment.

Application:

Ponder and prayerfully write about some of the "smallest" wrongs you can remember doing and still feel any guilt or shame or sorrow about. Write about whether this gives you some greater perspective on how tender and sensitive your spiritual self is. Can you begin to understand and let go of these things? Why or why not?

3.5 2 Nephi 31:13—Ye shall follow the Son, with full purpose of heart, acting no hypocrisy and no deception before God, but with real intent, repenting of your sins.

In the context in which this verse is found, Nephi is rehearsing to us the humility of the Savior (see verses 5-7 especially). The Savior had absolutely no need to go through such an outward demonstration of humility as baptism. Even so, though He was without sin, He humbled Himself before the Father and went to whatever lengths required to submit Himself to that process. So it is with us and the purpose of the fourth and fifth steps—there is no life too sinful or not sinful enough that cannot be made better by this act of humility.

Application:

The founders of Alcoholics Anonymous state:

> We beg of you to be fearless and thorough from the very start (*AA*, 58).

Being "fearless and thorough" in our inventory is absolutely supported by gospel principles and admonition. Prayerfully ponder **2 Nephi 31** and write about your willingness to go down into depths of humility to do a "fearless and thorough" inventory of your past. Write about the worst thing you could picture putting in such an inventory. Write about the most trivial wrong-doing you can remember. Think "thorough." Keep contemplating what that word means.

3.6 Jacob 3:7

One of the major things that will turn up in our inventory is how much of our present behavior is the result of the influence of our fathers (parents). Jacob indicates that the Lord is aware of this influence, and in His mercy, makes allowance for it.

Application:

The traditions which a set of parents pass on to their children are far more than just their outward celebrations or habits. Even more powerfully riveted upon the hearts of the children **(D&C 123:7)** are the "creeds" (beliefs) of the parents.

Prayerfully ponder the traditions of your parents. Make two lists of positive and negative traditions your parents passed on to you in each of three areas: in celebrations, in daily habits or routines, and in beliefs about self, life and others.

3.7 Alma 5:28—Behold, are ye stripped of pride? I say unto you, if ye are not ye are not prepared to meet God. Behold ye must prepare quickly.

This verse and the ones just before it are part of one of the most intense sets of inventory questions we could ever work through. They ask us if we have been **"sufficiently humble."**

As long as we continue to avoid living the spiritual principles of the fourth and fifth steps, we have not become *sufficiently* humble to avoid either relapsing into or switching addictions. Heart-deep recovery comes from a heart-deep willingness to be "rigorously honest."

> Both... pride and... fear beat [us] back every time [we try] to look within [ourselves]. Pride says, "You need not pass this way," and Fear says, "You dare not look!" But the testimony of [Twelve Step participants] who have really tried a moral inventory is that pride and fear of this sort turn out to be bogeymen, nothing else (*12&12*, 49).

Application:

Go to **Alma 5**. Prayerfully and carefully number and write out all the inventory questions Alma asks.

Write about how much better it is to be willing to live a life of honest self-inventory. Maybe you don't think it would be better. Why not?

Steps Four & Five—Week Four

4.1 Alma 12:14-15—For our words will condemn us, yea, all our works will condemn us; we shall not be found

spotless; and our thoughts will also condemn us; and in this awful state we shall not dare to look up to our God; and we would fain be glad if we could command the rocks and the mountains to fall upon us to hide us from his presence. But this cannot be; we must come forth and stand before him... he has all power to save every man that believeth on his name and bringeth forth fruit meet for repentance.

Our willingness to look honestly at our works, words, and thoughts brings us to the recognition of our need for Jesus Christ and His atonement. The fourth and fifth step inventory process is the equivalent of coming forth and standing before him. It is **"fruit meet for repentance."**

Application:

Prayerfully write about one time when you were not honest and you still haven't done anything to acknowledge that incident. Write about it (fourth step), find a willing friend and share it (fifth step). Record what the sharing experience was like. Did it bring you a sense of freedom and relief? Describe your feelings.

4.2 Mosiah 27:35—Zealously striving to repair all the injuries which they had done to the church, confessing all their sins, and publishing all the things which they had seen, and explaining the prophecies and the scriptures to all who desired to hear them.

Confession can also be a head start on the amends process. After giving away our inventory, making amends by confessing our wrongs to people we have hurt becomes easier. Every time we share a secret, it loses some of its power.

Application:

Prayerfully ponder and write about what it would mean if you were to strive "to repair all the injuries" you have done to others. What if you could find the power (grace) from the Lord to set aside your own injuries in order to humbly focus on any injuries you have done others? Write about whether or not you could accept that gift for even half an hour.

A possible way to word your willingness in prayer could be: "Lord, I pray for the power to set aside my defensiveness about injuries that have been done to me and to only concentrate on the injuries I've inflicted on others." Write about it.

> They always discovered that relief never came by confessing the sins of other people. Everybody had to confess his [or her] own (*12&12*, 56).
>
> Where other people were concerned, we had to drop the word "blame" from our speech and thought (*12&12*, 47).

Write your thoughts about how complaining about others and gossiping is a form of "confessing the sins of other people."

4.3 Moroni 6:8—But as oft as they repented and sought forgiveness, with real intent, they were forgiven.

This verse conveys the spirit of persuasion, long-suffering, gentleness, meekness, and love unfeigned **(D&C 121:41)** that God models for us. This does not mean that we can take advantage of His love, deliberately disobeying and then feigning (pretending) repentance. Notice the words "with real intent." Our intent must be real, or sincere. Many of us, however, if we were rigorously honest, would have to admit that we can identify with this statement:

> We have spent [a great deal of money and time] for examinations [from therapists, counselors, psychologists]… [Yet,] we have seldom told them the whole truth nor have we followed their advice. Unwilling to be honest with these sympathetic [people], we were honest with no one else (*AA*, 73).

Application:

Prayerfully ponder on this idea of "real intent." Try to remember a time when you pretended you felt one way about something, when in truth you didn't. How can fear of another person make you put on a facade and feign the opposite of what you know to be the real truth in your mind and heart? How does it feel to be false with another person? Have you ever done this with a therapist or other counselor or church leader?

Now ponder if there is any reason, ever, to be false with the Lord? To pretend anything? Why is it futile to pretend anything to the Lord? Write about it. Does it feel threatening or refreshing to you to think of being in the presence of Someone to whom you might as well admit your "real intent?" This is what it means to "bare your heart." Write about baring your heart to the Lord.

4.4 Helaman 5:17—Insomuch that they came forth and did confess their sins.

To bare our hearts to the Lord is good as far as it goes, but according to the principle of humility in the fifth step, it is *not* far enough. We must also "come forth" and confess our sins. We must come out of the closet, out of secret, out of that perverse form of pride called shame, and stand in the white light of truth. Shame is like a cancer. If even the tiniest bit of it is *knowingly*, intentionally, kept back from the "surgeon's knife" of Step Five, we will be prone to the "dis-ease" (lack of ease, of peace) that sooner or later results in a need to numb out again. This is often the reason we keep slipping and sliding, unable to find permanent release from our need to use.

> This is perhaps difficult—especially discussing our defects with another person. We think we have done well enough in admitting these things to ourselves. There is doubt about that. In actual practice, we usually find a solitary self-appraisal insufficient… If we skip this vital step, we may

> not overcome [our addictive behavior or challenge] (*AA*, 72).
>
> Most of us would declare that without a fearless admission of our defects to another human being we could not stay sober. It seems plain that the grace of God will not… expel our destructive obsessions until we are willing to try this (*12&12*, 56-57).

Application:

Prayerfully ponder your fourth step list. If there is anything on it that includes behavior serious enough—either legally or morally—to be confessed to a bishop or stake president and which you haven't taken care of, write about your thoughts, feelings, fears, willingness to do so now. If there is nothing of this nature on your inventory, make a list of others with whom you could do a fifth step and write about your inclinations towards sharing with each person on the list.

4.5 Ether 12:27, 37—And if men come unto me I will show unto them their weakness… And because thou hast seen thy weakness thou shalt be made strong.

These two verses are a good response for those moments when we are tempted, by either other people's opinions or by our own internal voices, to think that we are wrong to dwell so much on the negative. Doing the fourth and fifth step process is exactly the opposite of dwelling on negative things. As paradoxical as it may seem, facing our weaknesses actually gives us strength to overcome them.

Application:

Prayerfully ponder and write about the analogy of having an infected tooth or wound that you try to pretend you don't have. What are the results of not being willing and humble enough to admit you have such a problem? How is sin, which is harbored up and hidden, similar to these physical infections?

4.6 3 Nephi 1:25—Therefore in this same year were they brought to a knowledge of their error and did confess their faults.

Step Four brings us to a knowledge of our errors and the fifth step gives us an opportunity to confess.

> When we are honest with another person, it confirms that we have been honest with ourselves and with God (*12&12*, 60).

Application:

Prayerfully review your thoughts about giving your fifth step to another person. Pray for direction to the appropriate person. "Listen" to the impressions that come to your mind. Write about your fears and hopes surrounding each of them. Many people have some things to share for the first time, or to review more thoroughly, that need to be taken to a bishop or other church leader. Write about how you feel—comfortable or not—with your bishop. Could you explain the principle of thorough inventory to him? Write your thoughts out to yourself, first.

4.7 Alma 22:18—And I will give away all my sins to know thee.

> Even those who had faith already often become conscious of God as they never were before.... This feeling of being at one [peace] with God and man, this emerging from isolation through the open and honest sharing of our terrible burden of guilt [all our fears, resentments, and so forth] brings us to a resting place where we may prepare ourselves for the following Steps toward a full and meaningful [life of abstinence from addictive behavior] (*12&12*, 62).

Could there be more beautiful or powerful words spoken to capture the process of Steps Four through Seven? In Four we look honestly at our sins; in Five we talk honestly of our sins; in Six we become honestly willing to give them up to the Lord; and in Seven we honestly submit them to Him for His removal.

Application:

This is the last writing exercise for the fourth and fifth steps. Look back over the period you've been engaged in this study. How has it affected you? How much closer are you to understanding the gospel principles in inventory and confession?

Write a heart to heart letter to the Lord about your joy in doing this work or the fears that still hold you back. Listen for His comforting, strengthening, encouraging response. Translate the impressions of the Spirit into words and bear record in writing of His merciful kindness and patience.

Review the words of the hymn, "I Stand All Amazed" (*Hymns*, no. 193). They may supply the words of praise and awe your soul longs to express.

Supplemental Scriptures for Steps Four & Five

The following are additional scriptures which support Steps Four and Five:

1 Nephi 8: 5-7 Prayerfully ponder what it means that the follower of Christ is introduced into a **"dark and dreary waste."** Those who were valiant in the cause of Christ in the premortal life followed Christ into this fallen condition of mortality. In the light of this model, what might we expect to experience because we agreed to follow Him from the security and safety of our celestial home to participate in this plan of salvation and eternal growth?

1 Nephi 11:26 – Behold the condescension of God. This statement refers in part to every one of us, even as it does to the Lord Jesus Christ. Do we have the courage to look back at our **"dark and dreary waste"** experiences **(1 Nephi 8:7)**? Can I look back across my life – with all its mistakes and foolishness, with all its contributions to the challenges in this world—and see through it to my real self, who followed God to participate in a mortal, veiled, fallen, and temporarily confused existence? If I can, I'm finally ready to take Step Four in earnest—inventorying everything without shame or blame or need for denial.

1 Nephi 15:3 One portion of the truth that is especially **"hard to be understood"** (because we don't want to face it) is the truth about ourselves and what we are doing that is not good. We also tend not to genuinely see or believe what is *good* about ourselves, either. With every form of rationalization and justification, we avoid taking an honest look at our lives. We need to realize that it is the **"natural man" (Mosiah 3:19)** portion of us, not our truest and eternal self, that is resistant to spiritual truth. Nevertheless, we must be willing to **"look unto the Lord as** [we] **ought"** and be guided by the spirit which will teach us **"the truth of all things" (Moroni 10:5)**, including ourselves and our weaknesses **(Ether 12:27)**.

1 Nephi 16:26—And it came to pass that the voice of the Lord said unto him: Look upon the ball, and behold the things which are written. There is no required way to do a fourth step inventory, but almost all agree that some form of writing has been essential in seeing clearly what has been hidden. Every day, as we do another part of our inventory, we are able to look upon it and, seeing the things that have been written, become clear and balanced about our past. (Writing answers we receive to our prayers is also a way to watch the Lord's directions to us change from day to day.)

1 Nephi 17:41—He sent fiery flying serpents among them; and after they were bitten he prepared a way that

they might be healed; and the labor which they had to perform was to look; and because of the simpleness of the way, or the easiness of it, there were many who perished. Sometimes, we are tempted to be confused and put off by the fact that the Lord would allow "fiery flying serpents"—like experiences and habits—to make our earth-life so scary and challenging. We get caught in the lie that we must deal with all these challenges on our own. The truth is that He has only one purpose in allowing them to happen to us—to help us learn the true principles that will not only save us, but bring us to become even as He is. As we learn these principles and look to Him for healing through them, we must not let ourselves be distracted by other easier, softer ways.

1 Nephi 19:18—And I, Nephi, have written these things unto my people, that perhaps I might persuade them that they would remember the Lord their Redeemer. Nephi teaches us the importance of writing our own history and personal insights.

2 Nephi 4:17-18 Here is an example of a prophet of God being willing to be public about his weaknesses and sins. He's not only confessing to another human being, but to everyone who would ever read the Book of Mormon.

2 Nephi 30:17—There is nothing which is secret save it shall be revealed; there is no work of darkness save it shall be made manifest in the light. James Baldwin said, "Not everything that is faced can be changed, but nothing can be changed until it is faced" (*For Today*, 171). The first step to letting go of something is to bring it into the light.

Jacob 2:10—Under the glance of the piercing eye of the Almighty God. It is a hard thing to hear these kinds of phrases, but making God a witness of our fifth step is not just a formality, it is a necessity. Jacob is talking about his need, as the prophet to his people, to reveal the sins of others, but the same principles apply to us being willing to reveal our own.

Mosiah 16:1—Confess before God that his judgments are just. Sometimes, over our life's journey, we have made poor choices that have set us up for some pretty sorrowful consequences. In the process of all this, we often feel either consciously or unconsciously upset at life (that is, God) for how things went. In doing our fifth step—laying it all out to God—we are acknowledging that the consequences were understandable.

Alma 5:5 The Lord delivers people out of bondage **"by the power of his word."** "His word" is always synonymous with the truth. As we turn the cleansing light of truth on our past, we will be delivered out of the bondage of depression that the unacknowledged, unaddressed pain of our past has kept us in.

Alma 30:46—And now it came to pass that Alma said unto him: Behold, I am grieved because of the hardness of your heart, yea, that ye will still resist the spirit of the truth, that thy soul may be destroyed. When we resist the spirit of truth, we are resisting more than God. We are splitting away from our own deepest, truest self. You and I are, at our core, beings of **"the light of truth" (D&C 93:29)**. When we believe the lies of others about who we are—even when they don't mean to lie—we are being separated from the truth that God has taught us about ourselves. Which definition of us are we going to believe—the one given to us by other mortals or the one given by the Spirit of God? What we believe is a choice. If what we've been taught to believe is not bringing us genuine, lasting happiness, then we can deliberately choose to believe something different **(Alma 32: 27)**.

Alma 36:12-13 We are racked with torment only so long as we remember our sins without facing them. It's like knowing something is there but not being able to face it and find out. Once we do, we can honestly let go of the sin and even its memory. We will no longer be "harrowed up" by our memories. Instead we will actually be lifted up, when we come to realize that God's power to heal is greater than anyone else's power to hurt.

3 Nephi 17:14 While ministering to the Nephites in the flesh, Christ is **"troubled because of the wickedness of the people of the house of Israel."** That portion of His influence which is in our own hearts, usually called the light of Christ, is also troubled by wickedness. It is because of His Light, which each of us bear at the center of our hearts, that we are troubled by wickedness—both our own and also that which we have experienced at the hands of others.

We are beings of light and truth ourselves **(D&C 93:29)**. Thus even the smallest hidden act of darkness, harbored within our souls, torments and sickens us—spiritually, emotionally and often, even physically. Doing an inventory is the beginning of the end of that torment.

3 Nephi 28:36—I spake concerning those whom the Lord hath chosen, yea, even three who were caught up

into the heavens, that I knew not whether they were cleansed from mortality to immortality. Nephi uses an interesting verb, "cleansed," to describe the process of going from mortality to immortality. The miraculous thing is that we can begin this process even while in mortality. We can **"enter into the rest of the Lord from this time" (Moroni 7:3)** and we can be "quickened" (energized and enlivened) by a portion of the celestial glory while yet mortal **(D&C 88:29)**. We can begin this process by doing a thorough fourth step inventory. We will feel the Spirit more and more closely.

Other References for Step Four

As you find other references to Step Four in your personal daily scripture study, list them here:

Other References for Step Five

Step Six

Were entirely ready to have God remove all these defects of character. Became humble enough to yield our hearts and our lives to Christ for His sanctification and purification, relying wholly upon His merits, acknowledging even our own best efforts as unprofitable.

Most of us don't get this step when we first read it. I know I didn't. I skimmed across the surface of the words and exclaimed in exasperation, "Well, duh! Of course I'm ready to have this dang-diddly-darn addictive behavior removed!! No more compulsive eating—never, no way, na-da—never, ever again. And *now*, not tomorrow!"

There's just one problem with this kind of "let's get it done right now" attitude. It ignores the truths we learned in Steps 4 and 5—(1) that all the different forms of acting out we do are only *symptoms* of the heart-deep loneliness and confusion we all experience in this fallen world, and (2) God's intent in bringing us into recovery is not just to give us power to control the *symptoms* of the Fall. His intent is to *redeem* us from the Fall. His intent is to take us all the way to a mighty change—far mightier than any mere change of behavior.

God is all about changing our hearts—our character. You could say that His whole intent is to lift us up to a higher level of spiritual maturity through the experiences we have in this mortal probation, so that we can develop character traits more like His.

Until now, the steps have been about repentance. Step Six, however, is about realizing that while repentance is good, it only goes so far. It is not the crucial key to freedom from addiction. Step Six is about becoming ready to have the Savior *remit* our sins.

In this step, we prepare to shift the emphasis from our efforts to Christ's. We focus on the miracle of His grace, or power, to cleanse us from any interest in sin. It is where we realize that no matter how much we repent and prepare to be cleansed, it is only through *His* atoning power that we are actually made clean. In other words, we get ready to be still, and finally—finally—let *God* be the One who gets *all* the credit. We must get out of God's way and let Him change our disposition so that we have no more desire to sin in any form.

We are preparing to be changed. Not just a change of our outward behaviors, but truly changing our inner man. This step is about getting ready to have our lives changed at the heart-deep level. It's about becoming a whole new creature in Christ, being perfected in Him, *choosing* to become a son or daughter of Christ, being born again in His Spirit, and living at one with Him and with the Father.

This can be quite a long, drawn-out adventure. Why? Because the natural man has many deep and subtle ways to entice us back into trying one more effort to succeed on our own—without the Savior. Most of us take a lot of these detours—always leading to a dead end—before we finally realize we have no hope in changing ourselves. Our only hope is to come unto Christ in every single area of our lives.

Most of Us Do Some Addiction Switching Along the Way

One of the ways we avoid surrendering our entire character to the Lord is to take a few detours into one or more of the "socially acceptable" addictions. Many of us resort to "half measures" by switching to a softer addiction. If our original problem was something like alcohol, drugs, or sexual misbehavior, we may console ourselves with the idea that at least our over-spending or over-working isn't hurting anyone.

Switching addictions is an almost universal tactic among addicts in early recovery, so don't think you are a lost cause if you're doing it. We all try it, hoping it will spare us from having to honestly face the inclinations of our character, attitudes and beliefs that justify the use of our addictions.

Our merciful Savior knew we would try this kind of side-stepping. Gratefully, He allows many socially acceptable behaviors, such as overeating or perfectionism. The greater truth, however, is that a life of soft addiction is still not the best life the Lord has in mind for us. He wants to restore us to genuine sanity and serenity, so that we can eventually be free of *all* addictions. He wants to help us get down to the root causes of our troubles and troubled feelings. For that purpose, Step Six is essential.

Step Six marks a recovering addict's willingness to do more than just stop his addiction. It is the point where we admit our need for an "entire psychic change" (*AA*, xxvii).

> This is the Step that separates the men from the boys (*12&12*, 63).

This process of becoming ready for this mighty change of heart is spoken of in the Book of Mormon (see **Mosiah 5:2; Alma 5:12, 14**). It goes beyond the open heart surgery required in Steps Four and Five. Step Six prepares us for a *complete heart transplant*.

> **A new heart also will I give you, and a new spirit will I put within you: and I will take away the stony heart out of your flesh, and I will give you an heart of flesh (Ezekiel 36:26).**

How long does this heart transplant take? It depends on how stubbornly you cling to the heart you now have—the heart that's been hardened by the lies you've inherited from social customs and family traditions.

It's not your fault that you've been infected with these lies. It's not the fault of your parents or society either. The father of lies, the adversary of all hope and peace and joy, has been hard at work on the children of men since the beginning of human history. The Lord (and indeed, all of Heaven) eagerly awaits your readiness to stop trying to defeat the spiritual enemy of your soul with the psychological and medical approaches of mankind. He waits for you to turn to Him with all your heart, might, mind and strength, so that He can give you *His* power—the power to deny yourself of all ungodliness.

He has to wait a long time for some of us. Even after we've become abstinent from our original addiction, some of us continue to believe we can change our own hearts. It's as if we all have such a tendency to say, "Thanks, God, for removing my original problem—the behavior that was ruining my life. But, now that you've taken care of that, I'll take back the job of conquering the rest of my problems." Sorry, but it doesn't work that way. Step Six is the surrendering of all our self-sufficient pride and the receiving of the *gift* of a new heart.

Step Six can be understood by dividing it into three distinct parts, each marked by a key word. Most of us don't fully comprehend, or even hear, these key words when we skim past Step Six. Yet, they should trigger some heart-deep inventory questions.

Were *entirely* ready

Entirely. Am I really entirely willing to give up those defects or weaknesses in my character that keep me from partaking of the nature of Christ? What comfort or protection have these weaknesses given me? Am I ready to let that go?

to have *God* remove

God. Am I finally convinced that will power alone will not do it? That recovery only comes through God? Do I still think that setting a few more goals or making a few more promises will be enough? Or do I finally understand that I can't be rid of these defects until I'm willing to take them to God? Do I see that "No human being [resource] could…do the job" (*12&12*, 63)? Or am I still asking, "Do I really have to be that humble and self-disclosing? Look that foolish yet again?"

all these defects of *character*.

Character. Am I still trying to get rid of a few more bothersome *behaviors*? Or do I understand that my character needs a mighty change as well? If I'm *rigorously* honest, what tendencies and traits do I still see in myself that set me up for switching addictions? Do I really have to change this deeply? Can I?

Hopefully, reading, pondering, praying *and writing* about the following verses from the Book of Mormon will help to open the eyes of our understanding about Step Six and allow it to strip us of our pride (**Alma 5:28**) and bring us down into the deepest depths of humility we have ever known (**Mosiah 4:11**).

Step Six—Week One

1.1 Mosiah 3:19—For the natural man is an enemy to God, and has been from the fall of Adam, and will be, forever and ever, unless he yields...and becometh a saint through the atonement of Christ the Lord.

I struggled with my addictive behaviors for years, even after I had an absolute testimony that the Church of Jesus Christ of Latter-day Saints was all it claimed to be. Ever since my baptism, I have felt I could honestly say I *knew* that God lived, that Jesus was the Christ, that the Book of Mormon was true and that Joseph Smith was a prophet. And yet, despite all that, I could not stop the self-defeating, addictive things I did—overspending our checking account and charge cards, overeating until I was 50, then 100, and then 150 pounds overweight.

Why did I keep behaving like an enemy of good and of God, even though I had a testimony? It seemed that no matter how active I was in the Church, I still couldn't overcome the natural man—that part of me that, at the slightest temptation, totally forgot God and ran away to hide in addiction.

How could I be so two-faced? The adversary had me almost convinced that I was one of the worst liars, frauds and hypocrites in the world.

Then one day I was staggered by the description of an alcoholic who felt he had a deep, sincere belief in God, but could not get sober:

> While his religious convictions were very good… they did not spell the necessary vital spiritual experience (*AA*, 27).

I stared at this sentence, reading it over, as the Spirit translated it into familiar Latter-day Saint concepts: Having a testimony isn't the same thing as having a heart-deep *experience* with the *living* and vital presence of the Lord. It was another ten years before I finally had **"ears to hear"** and **"a heart to understand" (Mosiah 2:9)** this truth:

> Membership in the Church and conversion are not necessarily synonymous. Being converted and having a testimony are not necessarily the same thing either. A testimony comes when the Holy Ghost gives the earnest seeker a witness of the truth. A moving testimony vitalizes faith (Richard G. Scott, quoting Pres. Marion G. Romney, "Full Conversion Brings Happiness," *Ensign*, May 2002, 25).

Application:

Look up the words *conviction, vital* and *experience* in the dictionary. Copy any words or phrases you may find that would shed light on this difference between believing in the Church as contrasted with having a living experience with the Spirit of the Lord that converts or transforms all your priorities and affections.

Prayerfully ponder and write about your testimony or conviction about the Church and whether or not you feel that those convictions have been enough to accomplish a conversion of your inner self.

1.2 Moroni 7:3—You...that are the peaceable followers of Christ, and that have obtained a sufficient hope by which ye can enter into the rest of the Lord, from this time henceforth until ye shall rest with him in heaven.

Following Christ is a *peaceable* experience. It is not a gut-tight, white knuckle, striving experience. To truly follow Christ is to enter into the rest of the Lord—*right now,* not some time in the future. Once I have truly surrendered my life and my will to Jesus Christ, I can and will experience a sense of peace or rest, no matter what my outside circumstances may be.

In this state of inner peace, I will find my desire for my addiction either completely gone, or diminished to the point that I can let it go. When the desire starts to come back, when I begin to feel tense and my knuckles begin to get white, I know I have wandered too far from His Spirit and His rest.

Application:

Watch yourself for the next 24 hours. Make note of the times and circumstances that contribute to your tension and stress. Write about how the temptation to act out with your addiction increases in relation to your stress.

Instead of using a half-measure to deal with your tension, try deliberately meditating upon and capturing some scriptures that testify of the Savior. (If a particular verse does not come readily to mind, consider the following: **1 Nephi 11:7, Jacob 3:1, Omni 1:26, Mosiah 3:5, 3 Nephi 11:10-11, Mormon 1:15**.) How does meditation and capturing affect your tension and your temptation level?

1.3 1 Nephi 15:3—They being hard in their hearts, therefore they did not look unto the Lord as they ought.

Step Six involves looking to God "as we ought." In other words, looking to Him in all things, recognizing that it is only through *His* merits—not our own—that we are changed.

For most of us, this degree of surrender of self is extremely hard to do. Our hearts tend to be hardened with the universal sin of self-sufficient pride. Under its influence we are continually trying one "half-measure" after another, even though they "avail us nothing" (*AA*, 59). Eventually,we are humbled enough by our own repeated failure to change, to admit that "God is everything" (*AA*, 53), and that "there is [only] One who has all power—[and] that One is God" (*AA*, 59).

I sometimes wonder if there's anyone in all the world more proud and rebellious than myself. Even after being blessed with years of consistent recovery, I still find myself trying to deal with problems and weaknesses on my own instead of immediately seeking the Lord's grace.

I cannot believe how subtle and how quickly an attitude of "Oh, that's okay, Lord. I can handle this on my own, *without you*," can get started in me again. And when it does, look out! There goes my peace, my hope, my serenity—and my remission from the effects of sin. Oh, how easy it is to ebb back from "being entirely ready" to have God deliver me!

Application:

Prayerfully ponder and write about the process of becoming entirely ready—how it ebbs and flows, and how it can often involve a relapse into of pride. Think of a time when you've had strong resolve to never do it again (whatever "it" is for you) and then lost that resolve.

List the feelings that preceded your relapse or slip. Which negative thoughts are you most prone to believe? What character weaknesses do these tendencies reveal in you? Do you indulge in self-pity first? Or self-will? Self sufficiency? Self-right-ness? Or is it another self-centered feeling, such as resentment or bitterness, that shuts down your hope, faith and willingness to stay out of addiction?

1.4 Alma 32:28—If ye give place,…if ye do not cast it out by your unbelief, that ye will resist the Spirit of the Lord,…it beginneth to enlarge my soul;…to enlighten my understanding.

The seed of desire to become closer to the Lord, more like Him in thought, word and action, can be cast out by our own unbelief. All to often in my own Step Six process, I have cast out the seed of faith and returned to the false belief that God wouldn't help me until I got my act together and proved myself worthy. I came to realize that there is subtle but vital difference between trying to help myself (relying on *my* power) and trying to help Him help me (*His* power).

> If we ask, God will certainly forgive our derelictions. But in no case does He render us white as snow and keep us that way *without our cooperation* (12&12, 65; emphasis added).

In those hours when I am willing to be rendered white as snow by *Him*—believing that *He* can do this thing—I find *His* Spirit leading me, encouraging me, empowering me. In those hours when I don't want to cooperate by allowing Him to redeem me, He respects my agency and lets me go my own way again. This cycle of ebbing and flowing can be very discouraging, but it is a process we all go through as we become *entirely* willing to receive the success that God wants to gift to us.

Application:

Prayerfully ponder and write about how your ability to stay sober from your addictive behavior is "cast out" by an unbelieving attitude and thoughts like:

> "I don't believe I can do this," or
>
> "I don't believe the Lord can do this for me," or
>
> "I don't believe He *will* do this for me."

With which of these statements do you identify most? Do you use all of them to defeat your success? I know I have.

1.5 Ether 12:27—And if men come unto me I will show unto them their weakness.

These words shed light on one of the biggest reasons we back away from coming to the Savior with our weaknesses. We know in our heart that He won't just wink at them or brush them aside. Being the embodiment of all truth, He will show us the whole truth about our weakness in a degree of plainness we would rather not acknowledge.

As long as we put off coming to Him, we can still dabble in half measures, *trying* to get better, but never really recovering. We can still manage our own recovery. We can still determine which weaknesses we want to look at and work on. This hesitancy is part of becoming entirely ready. I can make it last as long as I hesitate.

> So, our troubles, we think, are basically of our own making.…There often seems no way of entirely getting rid of self without His aid. Many of us had moral and philosophical convictions galore, but we could not live up to them even though we would have liked to.…We had to have God's help (*AA*, 62).

Application:

Prayerfully ponder this scripture and write about your reluctance and resistance to see character weaknesses or tendencies, such as self-will, self-pity and resentment. How does it make you feel to face the fact that recovery is going to involve a heart-deep change of character—not just behavior?

1.6 Alma 45:16—The Lord cannot look upon sin with the least degree of allowance.

For years we have heard that God abhors the sin, but loves the sinner. This is true. God's love for each of us is unconditional—it has no conditions or requirements. Still, to become like God requires that we allow our character traits to be converted into traits identical to His own.

Those with Twelve Step experience will recognize what is often referred to as the Third Step Prayer, but it could just as accurately be a Sixth Step Prayer:

> "God, I offer myself to Thee—to build with me and to do with me as Thou wilt. Relieve me of the bondage of self, that I may better do Thy will. Take away my difficulties, that victory over them may bear witness to those I would help of Thy power, Thy Love, and Thy Way of life. May I do Thy will always!" We thought well before taking this step making sure we were ready; that we could at last abandon ourselves utterly to Him (*AA*, 63).

When we were taking Step Three, our "difficulties" were our foolish and insane behaviors, especially our addictions. In the process of Step Six, we realize that our "difficulties" are our character weaknesses. These difficulties are not removed until our dispositions are changed—until our hearts are changed.

Application:

Prayerfully ponder these thoughts: How terrifying, and yet thrilling, is it to know that God's intent is to perfect you, no matter how long it takes? How do you feel about *completely* abandoning yourself to God?

Write your own version of a Sixth Step prayer seeking total surrender.

1.7 3 Nephi 9:21—Behold, I have come unto the world to bring redemption unto the world, to save the world from sin.

The Lord declared this same message when He said:

> **And if any man hear my words, and believe not, I judge him not: for I came not to judge the world, but to save the world (John 12:47).**

My image of God made a mighty change when I read this verse of scripture and felt the Spirit witness to me that Christ's first and foremost purpose was not to judge me (at least, not yet), but to *save* me.

Suddenly, I understood that I didn't have to hide from Him while I desperately and futilely tried to get my act together. I did not need to fear that He would judge me negatively if He saw me as I was. He wasn't sitting at the *end* of my trail of tears and pain and mighty change, waiting to judge how well I had done slogging through it on my own. In Spirit and Truth, He was walking *with* me all along, suffering with me, saving me.

My Savior had given His life for the opportunity to be with me in my darkest hour, my deepest sin, my worst defects of behavior and of character. Why should I fear Him? Truly, I began to "enter upon a new relationship with my Creator," as a "new-found Friend" (*AA*, 13).

Application:

For the next several hours, allow yourself to imagine that the Lord is walking with you through your day.

Take the judgment gavel out of His hand and simply enjoy His saving presence.

Ponder and write about the difference between enjoying Him in your life as your Savior and your Friend, instead of as your Judge. How does it affect your behavior to receive the Savior in this manner?

Step Six—Week Two

2.1 Alma 36:15–16—That I might not be brought to stand in the presence of my God, to be judged of my deeds. And now, for three days and for three nights was I racked, even with the pains of a damned soul.

Alma's desire hide his deeds from the Lord kept him trapped for three days and three nights in a state of damnation, of hell. It is our own resistance to coming to the Lord—just the way we are—that keeps us trapped as well.

No! No! we cry. *There must be something else I can do, some other healing approach, some other therapist or program, some other procedure that can clean me up before I have to go to Him.*

As long we resist facing Him, we shut ourselves off from experiencing our own version of what Bill W. experienced when he finally chose to "turn in all things to the Father of Light who presides over us all" and received "a sense of victory,…I felt lifted up, as though a great clean wind of a mountain top blew through and through [me]" (*AA*, 14).

Application:

Metaphors, or comparisons, are powerful ways to understand true principles. For this exercise, picture yourself as a little child, about 18 months to two years old, who has discovered that a mud puddle makes a wonderfully mysterious and sensational place to play. What do you look like when your parent finds you ten minutes later? You could even throw in a dirty diaper and runny nose to finish off the picture! One thing is obvious, it's going to take a significant effort to get you cleaned up.

Prayerfully ponder and seek Heavenly Father's Spirit to guide your imagination as you liken your own need for recovery after having fallen into the mud puddle of this mortal world. Write about the way a loving parent would handle such a situation. Write about any desire you might feel to run away and hide from the Savior's efforts to find you and cleanse you.

2.2 **2 Nephi 4:17—Nevertheless, notwithstanding the great goodness of the Lord, in showing me his great and marvelous works, my heart exclaimeth: O wretched man that I am! Yea, my heart sorroweth because of my flesh; my soul grieveth because of mine iniquities.**

An almost universal reaction to coming to know the goodness and mercy of God is that we see the contrast between our fallen state and His perfected nature, and we feel ashamed and discouraged by the difference (see **Ether 12:27**). We may feel tempted to blame our actions on others, on the way they treated us in the past or how they treat us today. This is a natural response.

Through Step Six, we become ready to own the truth that we have been choosing to react to how they treated us. Accepting this truth is the culmination of the Step Six process. When we become willing to see the truth that our addiction has roots in our own character, rather than in others' treatment of us, we are finally ready to take Step Six.

Step Six is about getting past blaming others and making excuses. One woman expressed this attitude beautifully: "I am the result of the way I reacted to what happened to me" (*AA*, 544; emphasis original).

Application:

Prayerfully ponder and write about whether you're ready to own the following statement as your own truth: "What happened to me in my past helps explain my addictive behaviors, but it does not give me an excuse to keep resorting to those behaviors."

Make a list of those people or experiences from your past that you've been using as excuses to stay stuck on the merry-go-round of addiction.

2.3 Enos 1:2—And I will tell you of the *wrestle* which I had before God, before I received a remission of my sins. (emphasis added)

Enos describes the battle with his unrighteous desires as a "wrestle." Some of the ungodly character traits which we wrestle with are self sufficiency, self-will, self-pity, and self-right-ness. All of these are symptoms of the universal sin of pride.

This kind of deep, hidden pride can be so subtle and cunning that it can sometimes manifest as a reverse grandiosity, thinking of ourself as the best at being the worst. We think we are terminally unique, worse than anyone else.

However, when we are finally ready to come out from behind the lie of terminal uniqueness, we must become ruthless in our determination to be rid of our weaknesses of character, even as Bill Wilson described: "I ruthlessly faced my sins and became willing to have my new-found Friend take them away, root and branch" (*AA*, 13).

Application:

Prayerfully ponder and write about how you are doing on your journey out of addiction in general? Write about how closely (or not) you identify with the idea of "terminal uniqueness," or in other words, thinking that you're the best at being the worst.

Look up the word *ruthless* in the dictionary. Write out any part of the definition that fits your need to get ruthless with facing your sins.

2.4 Alma 8:10—Nevertheless Alma labored much in the spirit, *wrestling* with God in mighty prayer, that he would pour out his Spirit. (emphasis added)

Another Book of Mormon prophet uses the word *wrestle* to describe a period of struggle—in this case, with the Lord. As noted in the last exercise, the metaphor of wrestling is very appropriate to describe our struggle as addicts. Sometimes we're on top of our enemy, sometimes it's crushing our face into the mat.

When we find our way into recovery, we often feel like we've exercised all the strength in humility we can possibly muster while taking Steps One through Five. Then comes Step Six and yet another wrestling match begins, this time between our ego and God.

In our pride and ego, we insist on wrestling for the honor and the glory of our own recovery. We are very much like the drowning person fighting his would-be rescuer, rather than relaxing and allowing ourselves to be saved. Meanwhile the Lord wrestles with us to gain our wholehearted surrender of pride and ego.

Application:

Wrestling is a contact sport. To wrestle, we must get in close quarters with someone. Alma's way of getting in close quarters with the Lord was to come before Him in mighty prayer. This was also the way Enos made contact with the Lord—*conscious contact*.

Write about the interior tools of recovery (such as prayer, meditation, writing, literature study) and how they put you in close enough contact to actually wrestle with the Lord. How is this a sign of progress? How is it different from the times in your life when you avoided the Lord? Why do you think you're not willing to allow the Lord to win the struggle? After all, He is fighting for your salvation.

2.5 Alma 5:13—A mighty change was also wrought in their hearts, and they humbled themselves and put their trust in the true and living God.

The mighty change is not just a change in our behavior. It is a change in our character, in our hearts. As we go through the process of the mighty change, we begin to feel greater and greater willingness to trust God in all things, and our humility waxes stronger and stronger.

Application:

The powerful statement is made: "A.A. does not teach us how to handle our drinking…It teaches us how to handle sobriety" (*AA*, 553). In other words, these principles are not just to help us stop our addiction, they also help us face life without the addiction.

Prayerfully ponder and write about other problems in your life that you are beginning to consider asking the Lord to enter into and to change? Are you willing to let Him? Why? Why not?

2.6 Mosiah 4:29–30—And finally, I cannot tell you all the things whereby ye may commit sin; for there are divers ways and means, even so many that I cannot number them. But this much I can tell you, that if ye do not watch yourselves, and your thoughts, and your words, and your deeds…

This verse talks about the numberless ways we can sin. That might seem a discouraging bit of information to those of us longing for perfection. It is especially disconcerting to those of us who have spent a lifetime trying to muster the strength to overcome that one weakness that seems to rule the top of our list.

Thank goodness, Christ is not into behavior modification. The good news of the Gospel is that Jesus Christ is not a behaviorist! He is a heart surgeon. If we allow Him access to our hearts, He will perform an operation that will uproot the defects from which those numberless misbehaviors flow.

Application:

Prayerfully ponder and write about the contrast between the tedious, fruitless, futile nature of trying to overcome one sin at a time versus having the source of those sins cut out all at once. Can you hear the truth implied in the statement:

> No matter how far we have progressed, desires will always be found which oppose the grace of God (*12&12*, 66).

This statement does not say that *we* oppose the will of God. We want the same thing He does—getting ourselves straightened out and safely home to heaven. And yet we may still oppose His grace, His enabling power to gain and retain the gift of recovery. This verse talks of our need to watch our thoughts, words and deeds for all those ways in which we "oppose the grace of God."

How can we watch ourselves and also have an eye single to the Lord (see **3 Nephi 13:22**)? How would yielding our hearts and lives to Christ by counseling with Him in all our thoughts, words and deeds solve our problem of needing to watch ourselves and keep our eye single to Him at the same time **(Alma 37:37)**?

2.7 Alma 36:17—I remembered…one Jesus Christ, a Son of God, [who came] **to atone for the sins of the world.**

It was a great moment in my awakening when I got down off my high horse—the lie that I am more powerful to do wrong than God is to do good. Suddenly I saw that if He atoned for the sins of the world, then that included *my* sins, too.

In the next few verses **(18–19)**, Alma becomes ready to have Christ's Atonement applied to his life. He did this by coming to Christ, while still **"in the gall of bitterness, and…encircled about by the everlasting chains of death."**

Following Alma's example, we too can come to God while still in the gall of bitterness, while we are in the chains of addiction. The truth is that there is no other way we can come to Him. It is only after we come unto Him that He can break those chains for us.

Application:

The AA Big Book gives us a chilling statement about addiction:

> We are like men who have lost their legs; they never grow new ones (*AA*, 30).

In other words, there is no hope but to turn to God. No hope. None.

The Big Book goes on:

> Despite all we can say, many who are real [addicts] are not going to believe they are in that class. By every form of self-deception and experimentation, they will try to prove themselves exceptions (*AA*, 31).

And thus postpone turning to God for help.

Write a short story or scene in first person (where the main character is speaking directly to the reader), from the perspective of someone with a terrible disease who has refused to come to the Savior to be healed. What is the disease? Leprosy? Paralysis? Blindness?

In this scene, have your character finally become ready to approach the Lord. What stopped him/her before? What made him/her finally ready?

Stop now and write this story before reading the rest of the assignment.

Now that you have written your story, read it aloud, visualizing yourself as the person you've written about. Tell this story as if you are the one who is finally ready to come to the Lord to be healed. Write about how you felt while reading your story.

Step Six—Week Three

3.1 3 Nephi 24:3—And he shall sit as a refiner and purifier of silver; and he shall purify the sons of Levi, and purge them as gold and silver, that they may offer unto the Lord an offering in righteousness.

Have you ever experienced the joy of making a hand-crafted gift for a friend or loved one? Can you remember the excitement you felt, giving that gift? Your effort, your time, and your attention made it a very special gift.

This is how Jesus feels about you. We always hear about the gift He gave us, but have you ever considered that *you* are a gift He wants to present to our Heavenly Father?

You are His gift in process! He sits undistracted, purifying and refining you, awaiting the day when He will present you to His Father, like treasure, like gold and silver. This is His work and His glory. We are each His work and His glory. If we will allow

Him to refine us and shape us in His own image, He will present us to the Father, purified.

Application:

You have seen a perfect rose, a perfect sunset. But how about a perfect you? Is it possible? Prayerfully ponder and write about your desire to come to the Savior and permit Him to bring you through your trials and out of your weaknesses—to make you perfect.

Step Six is about becoming ready to surrender "all [our] faults—without any reservations whatever" (*12&12*, 63). Write about your willingness to give the Lord the gift of your unfinished, imperfect self so that He can refine and finish you and restore you to your heavenly home.

3.2 3 Nephi 18:32—Come unto me with full purpose of heart, and I shall heal [you].

This "full purpose of heart" is what Step Six is all about. It's a process. It takes time. Most of us try and fail at many "half measures" (*AA*, 59) before we are finally convinced that none of them will work.

We are taking Step One again, but at a deeper level. In Step One, we admitted we were powerless over external circumstances. In Step Six, we realize we are just as powerless over the world within ourselves. To be full of purpose as we come unto Christ is to be filled to the brim with the humble determination to let Him give us a mighty change of heart.

Application:

Prayerfully ponder and write about whether the words "and I shall heal you" create a stumbling block for you, keeping you from coming to Christ with full purpose of heart. Write about how the shame of having Him clean up your mess is keeping you resistant to the idea of coming to Him. After all, you're the one that sinned.

Or maybe your resistance is to the word "shall"—indicating that it may take some time for Him to bring this healing to pass. Explore in writing the possibility that you are feeling impatient with the process, wanting it to happen now or not at all.

Now, ponder on the word "you." Is your resistance to coming to Him based on the feeling that you are not redeemable, that you can't endure the process of being healed? Or do you hold some portion of your heart back from His healing, because you feel it is the other guy, and not you, that needs the healing.

Do any of these thoughts resonate in your heart and give you a clue as to what you're wrestling with? If you find you need help applying these exercises to your life, ask the Lord for counsel and comfort. He will give you both and help you to see what is holding you back.

3.3 Mosiah 5:7—Because of the covenant which ye have made ye shall be called the children of Christ, his sons, and his daughters; for behold, this day he hath

spiritually begotten you; for ye say that your hearts are changed through faith on his name.

> "Because of the covenant which ye have made..."
>
> "The children of Christ..."

Benjamin adds further validation to the expanded role of our Elder Brother, Jehovah, or Jesus Christ. He describes our covenant relationship with Christ as becoming His children, as begotten of Him. As we are willing to make and treasure our covenant with Him, we become born again, in His image—even as He is in the image of His (and our) Heavenly Father.

As we willingly take His image **"in** [our] **countenances" (Alma 5:14)**, we become His seed. In other words, He changes our hearts. He is the Father of our new birth, our mighty change. We cannot be born again, we cannot be recovered, without Him.

Application:

In looking up the word "begotten," I was led to the word "beget." Beget is a verb that refers to the act of a male parent, the equivalent of a female's act of conceiving. A mother conceives a child, a father begets a child. Both mean to give life.

Prayerfully ponder and write about your thoughts and feelings concerning Christ as a Father figure, as the One who gives you life.

3.4 Mosiah 15:10—And now I say unto you, who shall declare his generation? Behold, I say unto you, that when his soul has been made an offering for sin he shall see his seed. And now what say ye? And who shall be his seed?

At that moment when you became willing to allow Jesus to become an offering for your sins, He could finally see you as His seed, His child, His offspring, as explained in **Mosiah 5**.

While it is true that Heavenly Father is the Father of our spirits, Jesus Christ is the Father of our potential to recover; He is God's promise to recover us. I say "potential" because even though He has done everything necessary and within His power to ensure this relationship, it cannot become a reality without our desire and humble cooperation.

Application:

Prayerfully ponder and write about the two questions in this verse:

> And now what say ye, [insert your name here]?
>
> And who shall be His seed?

Will you become His seed? How do you feel when you see these words addressed to you, personally? Prayerfully ponder and write about your willingness to allow Him to be offered as a sacrifice for your sins.

For many of us, that is the most painful picture we can possibly imagine. But what alternative do we have, if we are to become His son or daughter and take His name (reputation) upon us? How far will our own reputation—fallen as we are—get us?

3.5 Helaman 13:6—Nothing can save this people save it be repentance and faith on the Lord Jesus Christ, who surely shall come into the world, and shall suffer many things and shall be slain for his people.

According to this verse, Christ was slain for "His people." I've come to realize that I am the one who gets to choose whether I am one of His people or not. And my choice has to be kept "new and everlasting" by always remembering Him, even as the sacrament prayers remind us.

In those hours when I don't remember to look to Him to guide my choices, I rapidly weaken and do not retain the remission His Spirit affords me. First, I start thinking faithless thoughts, then I start committing faithless acts. Soon I am returned to that bitter pain and anguish of sin. I am brought to remembrance again that **"wickedness never was happiness" (Alma 41:10).**

And from this place of pain, I again sincerely seek Him. With patience, long-suffering, and tenderness, He takes me back. By this process, by this combination of my foolish pride and His infinite mercy, I am becoming convinced to *always* remember Him. This is what it means to me to be "willing to go to any length" (*AA*, 58).

Application:

When you are in love with someone or looking forward to a upcoming event—a game or party or vacation—how often do you think of that thrilling person or that thrilling event during any given day? How does it feel to picture loving the Savior that much?

Prayerfully ponder and write about your willingness to take the Lord at His word in the Sacrament prayers, to always remember Him. Keep track of your waking hours for the next day or two. In how many hours of this day did your thoughts turn to Him or something about Him?

3.6 Alma 29:4—I know that he granteth unto men according to their desire, whether it be unto death or unto life…according to their wills.

Our desire, our will, is the determining factor in whether God will—or *can*—extend His power to us to endure our trials. He must wait for us to decide whether we are entirely ready to have both our behavior defects and our weaknesses of character removed. The moment we are ready, He removes them—or more accurately, transforms them into strengths in the image of His own character.

However, if we renege on our readiness, He must allow us to have our weaknesses back. Remission from our weaknesses is contingent upon what we desire most. We will always get what we desire most, both from hour to hour in our lives, and in the end as well.

The Twelve Step approach to recovery is so deeply grounded in the recognition and appreciation of the supreme importance of a person's own desires, that "a desire to stop" is recognized as the "only requirement for membership" (*12&12,* 139).

Application:

Prayerfully ponder and write about what you have believed concerning your desires. How comfortable do you feel expressing your own desires? How were your desires, wants, and needs treated when you were a little child? Were your desires respected, even if they weren't always met? Or did you develop the idea that other people's wants and needs and desires took precedence over yours?

Write about how you feel toward the Lord and His desires for you. What would happen if you decided to let Him and His will be your only desire?

3.7 Moroni 9:25—My son, be faithful in Christ;...may Christ lift thee up...and the hope of his glory and of eternal life, rest in your mind forever.

Step Six is all about getting ready to have Christ lift us up. It is letting go of any desire or temptation to feel our own glory. It is to become totally humble, to know and to acknowledge that it is by His power and His glory, alone, that we are saved.

Application:

This is yet another opportunity to keep Step One and Step Two current in our lives. We never outgrow our need to take Steps One and Two. Turn to page 233 to read Steps One and Two. Prayerfully ponder and write about any changes you have seen in yourself in practicing the first two steps. Has your willingness to admit that "all power and all wisdom" reside in God increased? If so, how? If not, why not?

Step Six—Week Four

4.1 Alma 14:26, 28—O Lord, give us strength according to our faith which is in Christ, even unto deliverance. And they broke the cords with which they were bound;…for the Lord had granted unto them power, according to their faith which was in Christ.

For many years I truly thought that strength to overcome my weaknesses (or sins or addictions) would come to me according to my own performances and efforts, according to knowledge of myself and my problem. Even after the Lord delivered me from my original addiction, I acted as if that's all He could, or would, deliver me from.

In this frame of mind, I spent untold time and money buying and reading books about my various challenges—my unhappy childhood, my codependency, my lack of organizational skills, etc. I ran from pillar to post and back again. "Lo here! Lo there!" Over and over again, I was blown about by every new theory of men which spoke to the problems I was focusing on. If I could just get a handle on myself, then I'd be able to conquer my weakness!

Then I read the following quotes from the AA Big Book and knew they were the truth—self-knowledge was not the end-all and cure-all I needed.

> Understanding myself now [because of a medical explanation of his alcoholism], I fared forth in high hope. [Three or four months of sobriety went by.] Surely this was the answer—self-knowledge.
>
> But it was not, for the frightful day came when I drank once more. The curve of my declining moral and bodily health fell off like a ski-jump ("Bill's Story," *AA*, 7).
>
> The actual or potential alcoholic [insert any label here], with hardly an exception, will be *absolutely unable to stop drinking* [insert any behavior here] *on the basis of self-knowledge*. This is a point we wish to emphasize and re-emphasize, to smash home upon our alcoholic readers as it has been revealed to us out of bitter experience (*AA*, 39; emphasis original).

Application:

Prayerfully ponder and write a list of the many ways or places you have sought answers, other than God. Include books, lectures, new plans, recovery programs and scientific theories you've turned to in the past. Have any of them provided lasting help? If they did, can you acknowledge the Lord's hand through these channels?

4.2 1 Nephi 3:7—Save *he* shall prepare a way for them that they may accomplish the thing which he commanded them (emphasis added).

This is one of the most quoted scriptures in the Church. We usually quote it as an example of great faith, but we seldom take note of just who it is that Nephi is expressing faith in. It wasn't just a general faith. Neither was it faith in himself. It was faith, *specifically* in God. Nephi knew "a way" would not only be *revealed* by God, it would also be *prepared* by God.

As stated earlier, Step Six "is the step that separates the men from the boys" (*12&12*, 63). As you go back and reread this verse and the surrounding story in the Book of Mormon, reflect on how Nephi's attitude made him a "man" as compared to his brothers, Laman and Lemuel, who behaved like "boys."

Application:

There are many paradoxes in the principles of redemption (recovery). Look up the word "paradox" in the dictionary and write the definition in your journal. Then prayerfully ponder and write about how one of the Gospel's greatest paradoxes is the need to "become as a little child" in order to become spiritually mature. How does this verse demonstrate

Nephi's childlike relationship with the Lord and his spiritual maturity at the same time?

Reflect on your willingness to let the Lord transform you into a spiritually mature man or woman. Reflect on your fear of becoming spiritually mature. Write about being willing to let Him make you **"a new creature"** in which **"all things"** will become new (see **2 Corinthians 5:17**).

4.3 2 Nephi 31:19—After ye have gotten into this strait and narrow path, I would ask if all is done?... Nay; for ye have not come thus far save it were by the word of Christ with unshaken faith in him.

With the ordinance of baptism, we make sacred covenants with God and enter the **"strait and narrow path."** Of course, that is not the end of our spiritual journey. While it is an event, it is only one event along our ongoing eternal path.

So it is with our recovery from a particular addictive behavior. Obtaining abstinence is usually marked by a certain date. A lot of recovering people speak of this as a birthday. Just like our baptismal date, it signifies that we've arrived at a new stage of life—not to stay at that level, but to go on.

As we continue to see underlying problems in our lives and continue to struggle with the adversities of this world, we must continue to **"[rely] wholly upon the merits of him who is mighty to save" (2 Nephi 31:19)** in order to move forward.

Many people get onto the path and then set up camp rather than begin the exciting, challenging—occasionally terrifying—journey into which Christ leads us. (See **1 Nephi 8:5–11** for the perfect model of our journey. Note that Christ first led Lehi into a **"dark and dreary waste."**) In recovery, things sometimes get worse before they get better.

Application:

If you have come this far in the study of the Twelve Steps, you have probably realized that it really is a program of *practicing*. The Twelve Steps are not a formula to immediate perfection. We continue on, "content with patient improvement" (*12&12*, 65).

Ponder and prayerfully write about your reaction to the idea of continual improvement. Do you feel frustrated? Or does the thought offer some relief in your struggle? Write about your reaction to any slips or relapses you've experienced. An old saying in Twelve Step recovery circles is, "You've got to love the process." What do you think of "the process"?

4.4 Moroni 10:32—Yea, come unto Christ and be perfected in him…then is *his* grace sufficient for you (emphasis added).

The key to our salvation couldn't be stated more plainly than it is in this verse. And yet, I skimmed right over it for years while I failed miserably at overcoming my weaknesses. I couldn't stop my addictive behavior and I couldn't stop the inner turmoil in my character—the self-pity and the self-will, the depression and the anger—all the feelings that set me up to use my addiction.

Only when I was willing to identify with a bunch of seemingly hopeless alcoholics, was I finally ready to admit complete defeat and come to Christ and allow Him to do for me (through His grace) what I couldn't do for myself.

> But my friend sat before me, and he made the point-blank declaration that *God had done for him what he could not do for himself.* His human will had failed (*AA*, 11; emphasis added).

Whether our character traits are inherited genetically, inherited socially, or have their roots all the way back into the premortal existence of our personalities as spirits—they are not within our power to change. They are rooted deep into the core of our souls, in our spiritual selves—and *only God* can change them. Only we can give Him permission to do so. Human will cannot change itself. It can only submit itself, surrender itself to be changed.

Application:

Prayerfully ponder and write about the excuses you've given for your weaknesses. Try to identify occasions when you've said things like, "Oh, I just have a temper like my grandpa" or "My parents were... That's why I..."

Read these two verses, slowly. Stop and write at least two or three sentences on every phrase. Write more if you feel like it. Let your thoughts and feelings flow, directed heavenward. Listen for answering thoughts. It is your privilege to have the Lord counsel you through the Spirit. You will know you have taken Step Six when you realize that you can find power in Christ to outlive any excuse.

4.5 Helaman 5:9—Remember that there is no other way nor means whereby man can be saved, only through the atoning blood of Jesus Christ, who shall come; yea, remember that he cometh to redeem the world.

For years I was totally oblivious to the absolute centrality of Jesus Christ in the Father's plan. I totally missed the fact that it was Jesus Christ who the Father had sent to be my Savior.

Thus, years of coming to the Father, even though I did it in the name of Christ, didn't unleash the Savior's power in my life. Like Alma, I had to also come to Christ and cry out to Him in my heart. I had to offer up my own equivalent of the plea, **"Oh Jesus, thou Son of God, have mercy on me…"** (see **Alma 36:18** and **Alma 38:8**).

Application:

Prayerfully ponder and write about what it means that **"there is no other way nor means whereby man can be saved" (Alma 38:9)**, except to allow Jesus Christ to become your dearest Loved One—even more dear to you than your parents, your spouse or your children.

Make a list of all the people you would think to turn to in a crisis before turning to the Lord. Write about what He can give you that they cannot.

4.6 Mormon 7:5—Believe in Jesus Christ, that he is the Son of God...whereby *he* hath gained the victory over the grave; and also in *him* is the sting of death swallowed up (emphasis added).

Victory over death and the grave, whether physical or spiritual (as in the bondage of addiction), is His and His alone. We only have as much victory as we will allow Him to share with us.

Application:

Prayerfully ponder this idea of the victory over your addiction and your character weaknesses as being the Lord's and *His* alone. Write a letter to Him expressing your willingness to be victorious by coming to Him and to the Father and living according to the Spirit. How do feelings of reluctance or resistance to doing this amount to pride?

4.7 Ether 12:41—And now, I would commend you to seek this Jesus of whom the prophets and apostles have written, that the grace of God the Father, and also the Lord Jesus Christ, and the Holy Ghost, which beareth record of them, may be and abide in you forever.

A few verses earlier in Ether, Moroni testifies to us that if we come to Christ, He will show unto us our weaknesses. It is the tendency of the natural man, the resistant part of each of us, to refuse to come to God in our weakness, but there is no other way to come to Him. We cannot overcome our incorrect thinking, nor the poor choices we make due to our thinking.

We have to come to the point where we know that

a. We are mortal, fallible, imperfect and weak, and cannot manage our lives well enough to save ourselves.

b. That, try as we might, we have not been able to find any human power that could relieve us of our addictive nature (natural man tendencies).

c. That God can and will, if He is sought.

(See *AA*, 60, for the original statements.)

Application:

Prayerfully ponder and write about whether you are ready to **"seek this Jesus of whom the prophets and apostles have written,"** right now, just as you are, with all of your character weaknesses, failings and deficits. Taking the next step, Step Seven, is going to mean just that: accepting yourself as *never, ever* being able to "get ready" to receive the Savior. It's time to let go of every ounce of pride and be completely without hope, except in Him. Are you finally ready to do that? Why or why not?

Supplemental Scriptures for Step Six

The following are additional scriptures which support Step Six:

1 Nephi 15:11—If ye will not harden your hearts, and ask me in faith, believing that ye shall receive, with diligence in keeping my commandments, surely these things shall be made known unto you. Pride hardens our hearts with such admirable attitudes as self-sufficiency and self-mastery, both of which, on a spiritual level, are deadly lies. Step Six is the process of digging deep into the roots of our pride.

1 Nephi 16:32—They did humble themselves before the Lord, and did give thanks unto him. Maintaining a grateful attitude can be a path to humility. How much better it is to be humbled by gratitude rather than compelled by adversity? Either way, humility always precedes the genuine willingness developed while working through Step Six.

Alma 12:10—He that will not harden his heart, to him is given the greater portion of the word, until it is given unto him to know the mysteries of God until he know them in full. Sometimes the greatest mysteries are just how far and how deep our own character weaknesses go. The mortal tendency to be in denial must be stripped away one layer at a time.

Alma 13:16—Now these ordinances were given after this manner, that thereby the people might look forward on the Son of God...for a remission of their sins, that they

might enter into the rest of the Lord. Everywhere, in our scriptures and in our ordinances, we are invited to "enter into the rest of the Lord," to stop fighting our own battles and allow Him to give us the victory.

Alma 23:7—They did lay down the weapons of their rebellion, that they did not fight against God any more. The weapons of our rebellion against God are our weaknesses or character defects. When we become willing to lay them down before the Lord, then we cease to fight against His will for us.

Helaman 5:47—Peace, peace be unto you, because of your faith in my Well Beloved, who was from the foundation of the world. God the Father knew from the beginning that this life would be so painful and so confusing that His children would become distracted. They would turn to false sources of strength and comfort. He called and ordained a Savior for us before the first person set foot on this earth. Our Father longs for us to turn to His Beloved Son for counsel and comfort.

3 Nephi 4:33—And their hearts were swollen with joy, unto the gushing out of many tears, because of the great goodness of God in delivering them out of the hands of their enemies; and they knew it was because of their repentance and their humility that they had been delivered from an everlasting destruction. Some of us try to avoid this step because of the emotion it inevitably stirs up. Tears are part of the cleansing process. They are evidence of honest emotion. We need not be ashamed of them or regret them. Taking Step Six usually involves the shedding of a lot of previously pent-up tears.

3 Nephi 6:13—Some were lifted up in pride, and others were exceedingly humble; some did...receive railing and persecution and all manner of afflictions, and would not turn and revile again, but were humble and penitent before God. Some of us feel justified in our "righteous" (even proud) anger. Others of us have learned that "resentment is infinitely grave…it is fatal" (*AA*, 66). Getting ready to let God have our resentment is part of the Step Six process.

3 Nephi 11:14—That ye may know that I am the God of Israel, and the God of the whole earth, and have been slain for the sins of the world. Christ had already achieved such a degree of knowledge and power that He could serve in the Godhead, as one with the Father. Yet, He willingly chose to descend to earth and take the role of the Messiah—not just to offer sacrifice, but to be that sacrifice for our sins.

3 Nephi 27:14—And my Father sent me that I might be lifted up upon the cross; and after that I had been lifted up upon the cross, that I might draw all men unto me. I hear in these words not just a statement, but a plea. "My Father sent me to do this work; please let me do it for you. Only when you let me do it for you, can I draw you unto me, empower you to be like me. If you resist my offering for your sin, I cannot spiritually beget you. I cannot make you my son or daughter."

Mormon 9:19—He ceaseth not to be God, and is a God of miracles. Christ performed many miracles of healing in His mortal ministry. Some were instantaneous. With others, He requested that the person do something—go and wash so many times or take up their bed. For some it was an event. For others, it was a process leading up to the event. Sort of like Step Six leading up to Step Seven. Whether it is a process or an event, or a little of both, we can trust that the Lord knows what combination will be the best for each of us.

Moroni 10:3—That ye would remember how merciful the Lord hath been unto the children of men, from the creation of Adam even down until the time that ye shall receive these things, and ponder it in your hearts. It was an important part of my recovery to start to notice all the *mercy* and *long-suffering* and *love* verses in the scriptures. They far outnumber the *wrath* and *punishment* verses, especially in the Book of Mormon. I began to believe that I, too, might find mercy in Him—not rejection or wrath. Steps Six and Seven were my act of accepting this truth about God: that while mercy cannot rob justice, it *can* satisfy justice, redeem my soul and make me sane (see **Alma 42:25** and **Alma 34:16**).

Moroni 10:6—Wherefore, nothing that is good denieth the Christ, but acknowledgeth that he is. In this day of general spiritual awakening, there are paths to healing and voices of sanity in a lot of places. As I negotiate my way through all these proposed ways and means of healing, I take this verse as my guide and avoid any program, product or person who feels adversarial or dismissing of Jesus Christ.

Other References for Step Six

As you find other references to Step Six in your personal daily scripture study, list them here:

Appendix

What Is Capturing?

What does "capture" mean? It means to get hold of something, really get hold of it, and make it your own. Here's how you capture thoughts from any source.

1. If your source is in the form of written material, underline the words or phrases that stand out to you. If it's in the form of a lecture, take notes as you listen. (Remember, taking notes is not the same as taking dictation. The goal is not to recreate every word the speaker says. The goal is to note those single thoughts that stand out to you.

   Most people think that this is the entire procedure, that this constitutes "capturing." Sorry. This is only the step of identifying what it is that you want to capture. (If you were an old-time cowboy and were sitting up on a ridge watching a herd of wild mustangs below you, just picking out the ones that look good to you is not the same as making them your own.)

2. Get a notebook of some sort (maybe a journal) and a pen and then rewrite the words, phrases, sentences or whatever you underlined or noted into that

notebook. When I copy quotes, I usually underline them as well as put quote marks around them so they stand out from the rest of what I write.

Now are you done? After all, you have written the thought down in your own notebook or journal. Sorry, this still does not make it your own. There is a third and final step. Without this last step you are only a collector of thoughts, not a captor.

3. Now write all that comes into your mind about the thought or quote that you have previously copied into your notebook. Why was it important to you? How did it connect for you? What does it say to you? How do you see that it applies to your life? This is capturing.

For me, this process of capturing thoughts, scriptures and quotes has also become a way of praying. I often find that I have just naturally entered into a prayer mode somewhere during this process, writing prayerful thoughts, expressing myself directly to God. And in just as easy and simple a manner I nearly always find myself realizing that what I am hearing in my thoughts is the voice of the Lord, through the Holy Spirit's mediation, speaking to my mind and heart.

(Colleen C. Harrison, *He Did Deliver Me from Bondage*, A-3 & 4)

THE TWELVE STEPS AS REFLECTED IN THE GOSPEL OF JESUS CHRIST

1. We admitted we were powerless over compulsive addictive behaviors*—that our lives had become unmanageable. *Admitted that we of ourselves are powerless, nothing without God. (Mosiah 4:5; Alma 26:12)*

2. Came to believe that a Power greater than ourselves could restore us to sanity. *Came to believe that God has all power and all wisdom and that in His strength we can do all things. (Mosiah 4:9; Alma 26:12)*

3. Made a decision to turn our will and our lives over to the care of God as we understood Him. *Made the decision to reconcile ourselves to the will of God, offer our whole souls as an offering unto Him, and trust Him in all things forever. (2 Nephi 10:24; Omni 1:26; Mosiah 3:19; 2 Nephi 4:34)*

4. Made a searching and fearless moral inventory of ourselves. *Made a searching and fearless written inventory of our past in order to thoroughly examine ourselves as to our pride and other weaknesses with the intent of recognizing our own carnal state and our need for Christ's Atonement. (Alma 15:17; Mosiah 4:2; Jacob 4:6–7; Ether 12:27)*

5. Admitted to God, to ourselves, and to another human being the exact nature of our wrongs. *Honestly shared this inventory with God and with another person, thus demonstrating the sincerity of our repentance, and our willingness to give away all our sins that we might know Him. (Mosiah 26:29; Alma 22:18)*

6. Were entirely ready to have God remove all these defects of character. *Became humble enough to yield our hearts and our lives to Christ for His sanctification and purification, relying wholly upon His merits, acknowledging even our own best efforts as unprofitable. (Helaman 3:35; 2 Nephi 31:19; Mosiah 2:20–21)*

7. Humbly asked Him to remove our shortcomings. *Humbly cried unto the Lord Jesus Christ in our hearts for a remission of sins that through His mercy and His grace we might experience a mighty change of heart, lose all disposition to do evil, and thus be encircled about in the arms of safety because of His great and last sacrifice. (Alma 36:18; Alma 38:8; Moroni 10:32; Mosiah 5:2; Alma 34:15–16)*

8. Made a list of all persons we had harmed and became willing to make amends to them all. *Made a list of all persons we had harmed and became willing to make restitution to all of them (even those we had harmed in what we might have considered righteous anger), desiring instead to be peacemakers and to do all that we could to come unto God by being first reconciled to others. (3 Nephi 12:9; 3 Nephi 12:24; 3 Nephi 12:44–45)*

9. Made direct amends to such people wherever possible except when to do so would injure them or others. *Made restitution directly to those we had harmed, confessing our own wrongdoing in each instance except when to do so would further injure them or others. (Mosiah 27:35; 3 Nephi 12:25; Mosiah 26:30)*

10. Continued to take personal inventory and when we were wrong promptly admitted it. *Realizing that the weakness to be tempted and to sin is a part of the mortal experience, we continued to take personal inventory and when we were wrong promptly admitted it, being willing to repent as often as needed. (2 Nephi 4:18; 2 Nephi 10:20; Mosiah 26:30)*

11. Sought through prayer and meditation to improve our conscious contact with God as we understood Him, praying only for knowledge of His will for us and the power to carry that out. *Sought through prayer and meditation to improve our conscious contact with God, seeking the words of Christ through the power of the Holy Ghost that they might tell us all things that we should do, praying only for a knowledge of His will for us and the power to carry that out. (2 Nephi 32:3; Alma 37:37; Helaman 10:4)*

12. Having had a spiritual awakening as the result of these steps, we tried to carry this message to others still suffering from the effects of compulsive behaviors and to practice these principles in all our affairs. *Having experienced a mighty change and having awakened unto God as a result of our sincere repentance demonstrated in taking these steps, we were willing to become instruments in carrying this message to others and to practice these principles in all our affairs. (Alma 5:7; Mosiah 27:36–37; Moroni 7:3)*

*Any problem may be inserted here.

The Twelve Steps have been reprinted and adapted with permission from Alcoholics Anonymous World Services, Inc. The opinions expressed are not to be attributed to Alcoholics Anonymous. The Twelve Steps of Heart t' Heart have been reprinted and adapted with permission from Heart t' Heart.

The Original Twelve Steps from Alcoholics Anonymous

1. We admitted we were powerless over alcohol—that our lives had become unmanageable.
2. Came to believe that a Power greater than ourselves could restore us to sanity.
3. Made a decision to turn our will and our lives over to the care of God as we understood Him.
4. Made a searching and fearless moral inventory of ourselves.
5. Admitted to God, to ourselves and to another human being the exact nature of our wrongs.
6. Were entirely ready to have God remove all these defects of character.
7. Humbly asked Him to remove our shortcomings.
8. Made a list of all persons we had harmed, and became willing to make amends to them all.
9. Made direct amends to such people wherever possible, except when to do so would injure them or others.
10. Continued to take personal inventory and when we were wrong promptly admitted it.
11. Sought through prayer and meditation to improve our conscious contact with God as we understood Him, praying only for knowledge of His will for us and the power to carry that out.
12. Having had a spiritual awakening as the result of these steps, we tried to carry this message to alcoholics, and to practice these principles in all our affairs.

BIBLIOGRAPHY

Alcoholics Anonymous, Alcoholics Anonymous World Services Inc, Fourth Edition, 1939-2001.

For Today

Pass It On: The Story of Bill Wilson and How the A.A. Message Reached the World, Alcoholics Anonymous World Services Inc; 9th edition, 1984.

Teachings of Ezra Taft Benson, Bookcraft Publications, 1988.

Teachings of the Prophet Joseph Smith, Deseret Book Co., 1977.

Twelve Steps and Twelve Traditions, Alcoholics Anonymous World Services Inc, 1952-2002.

About the Author

"Drugs, alcohol, food, work, perfectionism, spending money, gambling, destructive sexual behaviors, you name it, we're addicted to it. Being mortal and being addicted are almost synonymous," so says Colleen Harrison, a self-acknowledged recovering food addict. Colleen, mother of twelve children, has survived the death of her oldest daughter and the loss of her first marriage to addictive behavior.

Drawing on the power (grace) of Jesus Christ, Colleen has completed a B.A. and an M.A. in English at Brigham Young University. While at BYU, Colleen combined courses in psychology, human development and creative writing to create a uniquely LDS version of narrative therapy. "Writing—in a journal, on the back of an envelope, anywhere—is one of the cheapest and most powerful forms of therapy a person can use to recover from addiction, compulsion, or any other earth-life challenges."

Colleen moved to Logan, Utah in 1996, to pursue an advanced degree in Family and Human Development. However, after two and a half years of course-work toward a PhD, Colleen found herself in the midst of miraculous circumstances that culminated in her marriage to Philip Harrison. She has since retired from degree seeking status to better enjoy the blessing of "a marriage literally made in heaven" and to concentrate her energies on writing.

Colleen lives "after the manner of happiness" with her husband, Phil, in a cheerful, peaceful home which sees a continual stream of family (they have a combined total of 17 children and a growing number of grandchildren) and friends. Both Colleen and Phil devote their lives to carrying the message of sanity, security, and remission of sin through the principles of recovery expressed in these pages. You may write to Colleen c/o Hearthaven Publishing, P.O. Box 31, Hyrum, UT 84319.

Also by Colleen C. Harrison

ISBN: 978-1930738225
304 pages; 7.5 x 9.25; Softcover

Using the Book of Mormon and the Principles of the Gospel of Jesus Christ as They Correlate with the Twelve-Step Program to Overcome Compulsive/Addictive Behavior and Other Problems.

This book is about awakening, becoming a whole new creature in Christ by putting God first and developing a relationship with Him that is closer and sweeter than any other. It's about being delivered from the bondage of lies, recovered by the Spirit of Truth, Jesus Christ. Originally published in 1991, and now in a 20th Anniversary edition, *He Did Deliver Me from Bondage* has become the number one best-selling LDS Twelve Step Recovery book.

Fire changes things. Absolutely, molecularly. Writing under fire does the same thing.

Colleen Harrison grew up believing in God. She found Him in the loneliness of a neglected childhood, felt His comfort and protection during the violent outbursts of her parents' relationship, and experienced His strength, hope and healing amidst some of life's hardest trials. Through it all, Colleen finds and shares with us one overarching truth: the gospel of Jesus Christ works.

ISBN: 978-1930738164
174 pages; 6x9; Softcover

Also from Hearthaven Publishing

An LDS Twelve Step Guide
to Overcoming Addiction
to Pornography through the
Redeeming Power of Jesus Christ

ISBN: 978-1930738195
312 pages; 6x9; Softcover

Using the scriptures and teachings of Church leaders, along with the Twelve Steps of recovery, Philip A. Harrison leads us through the process of coming unto Christ and having our burdens lifted. For those who have struggled with sexual addiction or any other overwhelming challenge, as well as for those who care about them, this book offers welcome help, guidance and hope.

ISBN: 978-1930738218
226 pages; 6x9; Softcover

At Last—Help for the Spouses
of Sex Addicts

Do you have a loved one who is sexually addicted? Do you wish you could visit with a couple who has faced this challenge and survived?

Colleen and Phil share the principles and insights that helped them find the Savior's grace and guidance to face and survive the heartache of sexual addiction. Their combined testimony is that you can find peace and healing through the Savior's offer of atonement.

www.hearthavenpublishing.com

Patterns of Light, Vol 1 Journal Pages

A downloadable and printable companion .pdf document makes it easy to journal each day's study question as you read through Patterns of Light, Volume 1.

Single-sided, full-size 8.5 x 11″ pages contain the study questions from the book with lines for your answers. Plus blank lined pages to extend your journaling. Find it at:

www.shop.hearthavenpublishing.com

Free Scripture Marking Chart

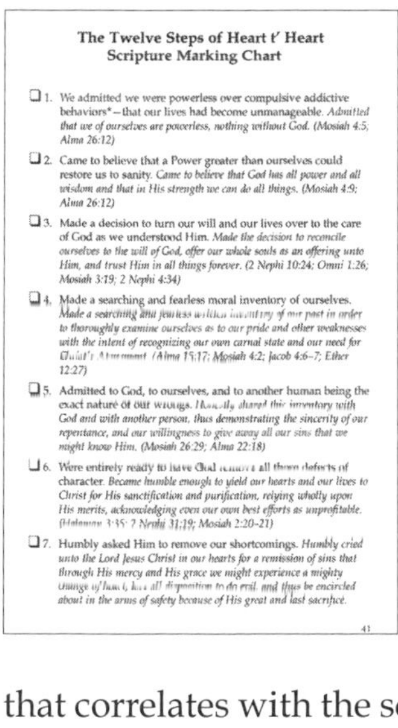

The Twelve Steps of Heart t' Heart Scripture Marking Chart

- ❑ 1. We admitted we were powerless over compulsive addictive behaviors*—that our lives had become unmanageable. *Admitted that we of ourselves are powerless, nothing without God. (Mosiah 4:5; Alma 26:12)*
- ❑ 2. Came to believe that a Power greater than ourselves could restore us to sanity. *Came to believe that God has all power and all wisdom and that in His strength we can do all things. (Mosiah 4:9; Alma 26:12)*
- ❑ 3. Made a decision to turn our will and our lives over to the care of God as we understood Him. *Made the decision to reconcile ourselves to the will of God, offer our whole souls as an offering unto Him, and trust Him in all things forever. (2 Nephi 10:24; Omni 1:26; Mosiah 3:19; 2 Nephi 4:34)*
- ❑ 4. Made a searching and fearless moral inventory of ourselves. *Made a searching and fearless [illegible] of our past in order to thoroughly examine ourselves as to our pride and other weaknesses with the intent of recognizing our own carnal state and our need for [illegible] (Alma 15:17; Mosiah 4:2; Jacob 4:6–7; Ether 12:27)*
- ❑ 5. Admitted to God, to ourselves, and to another human being the exact nature of our wrongs. *[illegible] this inventory with God and with another person, thus demonstrating the sincerity of our repentance, and our willingness to give away all our sins that we might know Him. (Mosiah 26:29; Alma 22:18)*
- ❑ 6. Were entirely ready to have God [illegible] all these defects of character. *Became humble enough to yield our hearts and our lives to Christ for His sanctification and purification, relying wholly upon His merits, acknowledging even our own best efforts as unprofitable. ([illegible] 3:35; 2 Nephi 31:19; Mosiah 2:20–21)*
- ❑ 7. Humbly asked Him to remove our shortcomings. *Humbly cried unto the Lord Jesus Christ in our hearts for a remission of sins that through His mercy and His grace we might experience a mighty [illegible] all disposition to do evil, and thus be encircled about in the arms of safety because of His great and last sacrifice.*

41

Use our Scripture Marking Chart to correlate the Twelve Steps with the scriptures.

Download the free pdf from our website. Copy the chart onto white cardstock, double-sided; then cut in half. (Makes two.)

Select a different color plastic scripture-marking crayon or colored pencil for each step. Color in the boxes on the chart with the corresponding color for that step.

As you study the scriptures, mark the verses with the color of the step that correlates with the scripture. Some people choose to mark the scripture itself, while others choose to make a dot or square of color in the margin by the scripture.

www.shop.hearthavenpublishing.com/freebies